SATAN SPEAKS!

CONTEMPORARY SATANIC VOICES

A Forty-Two Books, LLC. original publication,
Salt Lake City, UT.
www.fortytwobooks.com

ISBN-13: 978-1-7340067-1-1
Library of Congress Control Number:
2019913434

Printed in USA on acid free paper.

Editor

Faustus Blackbook, MA

First Edition. First Printing

SATAN SPEAKS!

CONTEMPORARY SATANIC VOICES

OCTOBER 2019

EDITED BY FAUSTUS BLACKBOOK

42

Books

Salt Lake City

Titles Available from Forty—Two Books

Peaks of Madness: A Collection of Utah Horror
Published April 2019, $19.99, 364 pages of original Utah horror by the Utah Horror Writers

Putrescent Poems: Horror Poetry Vol 1,
Published October 2019, $17.99, 90 page hardcover of original horror poetry.

Forthcoming Titles from Forty—Two Books

2019

Strange Stories Vol 1 edited by Daniel Cureton, Amy Pittman, and Kylie Williamson

Monster Brain: Conversations with OCD by Daniel Cureton

2020

They Walk Among Us: A Collection of Utah Horror by the Utah Horror Writers.

All Titles Available on Amazon.com or from Forty-Two Books

Letter from the Editor

ꕥ + ꕥ

It was my goal to collect the voices of the contemporary Satanic community. Here in this volume I have tried my best to faithfully represent the diverse narratives from across the world. I greatly enjoyed the authors with which I worked, editing their stories, essays, and poetry to bring it up to the standards for publication at Forty-Two Books in Salt Lake City. It is inclusive of all Satanic paths, not respecting one or nodding to one more than another (including the title).

Thank you to Mr. Daniel Cureton for graciously making a home for these forgotten, marginalized, and outcast voices.

Ave Satanas,
Faustus Blackbook,
October 1, 2019
Utah, USA

Introduction from the Publisher

ꕥ + ꕥ

I had the great pleasure of working with Faustus on this unique and needed project. As a publisher, I have set myself up to publish the weird, the transgressive, and the outcast in the world. I have always wanted to build a bigger sandbox for everyone, and one of my own research interests is minority cultural voices, and Satanism is exactly it!

Faustus approached me some time ago about the project after I had the company up. I happily agreed, indicating that it would be a fun and interesting project to take on. I know there would be a community receptive to it in Utah as they tend to be open to things of which they aren't aware.

We received over thirty submissions from around the world. This anthology is an international work in the field, not rejecting based on national origin, but purely on craft and form. Extra strides were taken by Faustus to work with authors to include them in this groundbreaking anthology, spending much time editing and revising so that the voice of contemporary Satanism is accurately represented but still bears high quality writing.

Included are authors from India, New Zealand, England, Canada, Italy, and the USA. Where appropriate, bilingual versions of works have been included.

This symbol -» means the work continues onto the next page.

It is my aim as publisher to present to the world this first collection of Satanic voices. This is in no way pushing an agenda, but creating a safe space for an often forgotten and excluded community of humans.

I present to you:

SATAN SPEAKS!

In Satan,
Daniel Cureton, MA
October 1, 2019
Salt Lake City, UT, USA

Catalogue of Satanic Combinations

Part 1 - Essays

Part 2 - Creative Nonfiction

CATALOGUE

PART 3—POETRY

Part 4 - Short Fiction

CATALOGUE

Author Biographies

Baron Henderson is a writer living and working in Utah.

Bruce McRae, a Canadian musician currently residing on Salt Spring Island, BC, is a multiple Pushcart nominee with over 1,500 poems published internationally in magazines such as *Poetry*, *Rattle* and the *North American Review*. His books are *The So-Called Sonnets* (Silenced Press), *An Unbecoming Fit Of Frenzy* (Cawing Crow Press), L*ike As If* (Pski's Porch), and *Hearsay* (The Poet's Haven).

Coventree has dabbled at writing for over twenty years in the U.S. with articles appearing in various magazines and newspapers. Recently using a creative mind, Coventree moved into poetry and finds the switch refreshing. As a creative person, Coventree sees the world from different perspectives and allows space for all types of diversity.

Ed Ahern resumed writing after forty odd years in foreign intelligence and international sales. He's had over two hundred fifty stories and poems published, and five books. Ed works the oth-

er side of writing at Bewildering Stories, where he sits on the review board and manages a posse of five review editors. Ed writes frequently on the occult, using his own library of 150 books on the supernatural and demonic. Follow him at
https://twitter.com/bottomstripper

Eskarina Weatherwax is an old time writer and poet living in Utah. Hailing from Southern California, she enjoys hiking with her husband.

Faustus Blackbook is a Satanist hailing from Utah. Having moved there in 2008, he quickly found himself an outcast and sought sinister friends. He is a member of The Satanic Temple and has a Master's in English.

Federico Federici lives between Berlin and the Ligurian Apennines. His works have appeared in international journals and anthologies including *3:AM Magazine*, *Jahrbuch Der Lyrik*, *Poet Lore*, *Raum*, and *Trafika Europe*. Among his books is prose and poems in English and German *Requiem auf Einer Stele* (2017), the asemic albums *Liner notes for a Pithecanthropus Erectus Sketchbook* (2018) and *A Private Notebook of Winds* (2019). In 2019 he was awarded the Nassau Review Writer Awards for poetry.

Federico Federici vive tra Berlino e l'Appennino ligure. Suoi contributi e testi sono comparsi su riviste e antologie internazionali quali *3:AM Magazine*, *Jahrbuch Der Lyrik*, *Poet Lore*, *Raum*, e *Trafika Europe* e altre. Tra i libri "*Requiem uf Einer Stele*" (2017) opera in poesia e prosa bilingue (inglese e tedesco), l'album di scritture asemiche *Liner Notes for a Pithecanthropus Erectus Sketchbook* (2018) con prefazione di SJ Fowler e *A Private Notebook of Winds* (2019). Nel 2019 ha vinto il Nassau Review Writer Awards per la poesia.

J. Barrett Wolf has been writing for over forty years. He has received numerous awards, including First Place from the Performance Poets Association of Nassau County and a Broome County Arts Council grant to produce the reading series "Here & There: Poets from Near and Far." He's been published in *Black Bear Review*, *Portland Review of the Arts*, *Long Island Sounds*, *Rubber Side Down*, *PPA Literary Review*, and *Writing Outside the Lines*. His first volume, *Stark Raving Calm* was published by Boone's Dock Press.

Janine Mercer's work has been featured in *The Quint, Sinister Wisdom*, *The Cardinal Stritch*

University Magazine, and others. She currently resides in Milwaukee, WI with her wife and a moderately creepy collection of taxidermy. Her current projects include two podcasts, The Vanishing Hitchhiker and The Oddentity Podcast (oddentitypod.podbean.com) and a lit rag called *Corvus Review* (www.corev.ink) She holds a B.A. in Writing and Communication from Cardinal Stritch University in Milwaukee, WI and will soon receive her MFA in Creative Writing from the Jack Kerouac School of Disembodied Poetics from Naropa University in Boulder, CO.

Jessica Thomas is an emerging writer and illustrator living in New Zealand. She writes middle grade fiction, poetry, and has published several articles on the understanding and practice of witchcraft, both past and present, and is actively involved in academic discussions of gothic literature. Jessica completed a Masters in History, specializing in medieval medicine. Her poetry been published in university journals and she is currently working on an anthology of further gothic and absurd poems and short stories.

Jim Piatt is an American writer who by adornment acknowledgers his own ugliness.

Mark Blickley is a proud member of the Dramatists Guild and PEN American Center and recipient of a MacArthur Foundation Scholarship Award for Drama. He is the author of *Sacred Misfits* (Red Hen Press) and a 2018 Audie Award finalist for his contribution to the original audio book, *Nevertheless We Persisted.* Last year his video, *Widow's Peek: The Kiss of Death,* was selected to the International Experimental Film Festival in Bilbao, Spain.

Mark Andrew Heathcote is from Manchester in the UK, author of *In Perpetuity* and *Back on Earth,* two books of poems published by a CTU (Creative Talents Unleashed) publishing group find out more: www.ctupublishinggroup.com/mark-andrew-heathcote.html

Matt Skaggs is a musician and poet local to Salt Lake City. His writing is heavily influenced by the works of Tom Waits and Nick Cave. A firm atheist and skeptic, Matt appreciates the use of "the adversary" as a way to shine a light on religious hypocrisy and fight against ignorance. He also enjoys long walks on the beach, writing bad haikus, and cooking.

Michal Mahgerefteh is an artist and poet from

Norfolk, Virginia. She is the author of four poetry chapbooks: *In My Bustan*, *What's Left Behind*, *Field of Harps,* and *Sipping Memories*. Michal is the managing editor of *Poetica Magazine*, *Mizmor Anthology* and the Anna Davidson Rosenberg Poetry Award. Her poetry has been published and anthologies, most recent in The 2019 *Voices Israel Anthology, Tiger Moth Review*, *The Ekprastic Review*, and *The Jewish Literary Review.*

Misako Yamazaki is a 22-year-old is a future college professor. Phoenix born and raised, she has self-published *Wasps: (And Other Poems)*, and is a connoisseur of all things literary. She is currently studying towards her BA in Philosophy, Religion and Society at Barrett, The Honors College at Arizona State University. She is also a part-time Student Success Specialist and the founder and president of Spilled Ink Club at Phoenix College. A slam poet, Misako spends her free time reading, writing, and journaling.

Neil Rhind was doctored in Literature from Edinburgh in 2009. His work has been published in *The Scottish Literary Review*, *The International Review of Scottish Studies*, and *The International*

Journal of Scottish Literature and was recently anthologised in *Spectral Lines: Poems About Scientists* [Alternating Current Press]. He commits ritually significant things in Edinburgh, and is into the Fall (season) and the Fall (band) but not the Fall (existential state of Damnation).

P.W. Covington writes in the Beat tradition of the North American highway. His latest book, *North Beach and Other Stories,* a collection of short fiction and erotica, was named a 2019 Finalist by the International Book Awards. He lives in Northern New Mexico, two blocks off of Historic Route 66. Follow him @BeatPW on Insta.

Richard Schiffman is an environmental journalist, poet and author of two biographies. His poems have been published in the *Alaska Quarterly*, *The New Ohio Review*, *The New York Times*, *Writer's Almanac*, and many other publications. His first poetry collection *What the Dust Doesn't Know* was published in 2017 by Salmon Poetry. He does not believe in the literal existence of the Devil, but regards Satan as the embodiment of human ignorance.

R. Keith's interests lie in philosophy, atheism, poetics, fiction, visual art. He is the author of twenty books, twelve of which he published in one year. Latest publications include *Wild Rose Country* (Cajun Mutt Press), *Flop* (Rust Belt Press), *A Polemic Study of Negative Space* (Ma Press), and forthcoming *Around the Bend* (Cajun Mutt Press).

Sravani Singampalli is a writer, poet and artist from India. Her works are published and or forthcoming in *Kaleidoscope, Parks and Points*, Deaf Poets Society, Purple Fire Publications, *Alban Lake*, *Treehouse Arts*, *House of Zolo*, *Blind Faith Magazine* and many more. She is presently pursuing a doctoral degree in pharmacy at Jntu Kinada university in Andhra Pradesh, India. Apart from writing, she likes drawing and painting in her spare time. She is very fond of House Sparrows.

Thursday Simpson lives between Iowa City, Iowa and Peoria, Illinois. She has a BA from the University of Iowa. Thursday identifies as a Queer Satanic Witch, a Satanic Hermit, and a multimedia artist. Her first multimedia collection, *Three Gothic Stories*, is available at Moonchaps via *Moonchild Magazine*. Thursday's work has also recently been anthologized in *Nasty! Volume 2* and *Hexing the Patriarchy*. Her full publication history is available online for viewing at her website, www.thursdaysimpson.com

THE SATANIC COMBINATIONS

PART I

ESSAYS

New Objectivism: Satanic Though

+

Faustus Blackbook

In the 21st century, it seems that the ocean of information is as polluted as the real oceans of Earth. The masses can no longer be relied on to sift through the petabytes of data available, much less understand, interpret, and use the information they need (Seminole State Library). Commonly known as information literacy in library science (ALA), the problems stems from the instant access and digital mediums which make the information world ever more subtle and covert

With the distrust of information, the breaking the American public into tribal political camps, and the disregard for the empirical processes of science, a new form of thought is needed—New Objectivism: Satanic Thought. This is far from the LaVeyian days that strode to detach from dominate Christian structures, but more in the field of intellectualism.

With the world of information always available, much isn't left to shock the masses. The LGBTQ Stonewall Riots of 1969 (A&E), filth exploitation films of the 1970s (i.e John Waters' *Multiple Maniacs* (1970), Michael Findlay's *Snuff* (1976)), satanic panic of the 1980s (Romano), and the recent Gender Revolution of 2017 (Goldberg) have all come to a calm life that exists among the public discourse and those who value it, take comfort in them.

21st century Satanism, doing its job by litigating in courts and challenging state legislatures for passing theocratic laws, seems to be one of the few avenues left to shake the public's consciousness, rile up the conservatives, and effect actual change where the traditional dialogue and science has failed to penetrate.

This is not to dismiss the great need and power of the dialogue, and of empirical scientific practices and data, but the indoctrination of the "fake news" (Smith) culture has disenchanted those who were on the fence about the conversations taking place and pushed those already against science further into their own camps (Coll).

While those people can claim the reports

and evidence are falsified, what challenges can they make to Satanism? There is no ancient claim to the origin, the ideas of Satanism simply exist as a faith made up to serve a particular need in a society in a defined time period. All faiths, regardless of origin, are based solely on the beliefs of its followers. Without such belief, the active faith fades into history and the canonical texts are shelved.

Far too often have the representatives and senators been allowed to erect monuments of the Ten Commandments in defense that it's the foundation of American jurisprudence or the foundation of America itself (Chappell). These representatives are doing the same thing in their states and countries which they abhor in other countries with non-Christian religious rule—enshrining into law for the masses a theocratic structure which seeks only to further that theocracy—the irony is not lost on those who have left the dogma box.

Since the underpinning impetus for the Satanic movement was to break away from oppressive structures of these types, figures like Anton LaVey knew quite well that they were making it up as they went along.

> It was more about rational freethinking and a disdain for the hypocrisy he believed corrupted Christianity.
>
> He preached living for the day, instead of for an afterlife that nobody can prove exists, they said. He did not believe in the devil as an anthropomorphic being with horns and a tail, but rather as a Jungian archetype conjured up by mankind (Washington Post).

Far from the occultist who claim they work with demons and lords of hell, Satanism's own meta acknowledgement that "It's called Satanism because there's nothing else to call it," (Greaves (Morgenstern)) gives it the power to acts as an objective mechanism from which new narratives, new dialogues, and quick actions can originate.

New Objectivism is a term I am giving this new wave of intellectualism within Satanism—the wave which seeks data, science, peace, and equality over the Satanic stunts performed in the 20th century. This updated term is necessary since our societies have evolved and it was time for the faith and movement to evolve with it. Satanism can serve as the basic objectivism by evidence driven humans.

This sounds like an obvious statement, and the question posed about new objectivism needs to be discussed: "Why does new objectivism need to be Satanic." Simply put, it does not. Any person can arrive at a parallel way of thinking through the influence of science and scholarly practices, being open to dialogue and criticism, which push them generally into being more open and accepting in the world, but this essay is aimed at those whom have yet to arrive there and need to understand how objective thought can be incorporated into Satanic life, especially considering that for the masses, science and the academy is elitist and set out to corrupt young minds to liberalism (Shapiro).

At least for The Satanic Temple, the foundation for thought is based on a study of literature and literary scholarship using Satan as an archetype of rebellion against the story's protagonist (The Satanic Temple); 21st century Satanism is operating in the same manner. Stepping away from the activism and protests, the base line of Satanism today is an attempt to come onto the same terms/common ground with the people whom we seek to enlighten. The wall that is thrown up by the non-Satanist (by Satanists quoting data/facts) can be scaled by understanding their side and helping them to overcome the negative rhetoric on which they have been programmed (much like the rest of us), especially since there is no dogma which serves as the singularity of irreconcilable difference.

Knowledge and discourse can effect change in the world. While other dialogues falls on deaf ears (a broken record), Satanism is protected in the USA (Bell) among other countries, making it an open road. Like LaVey knew, the movement isn't bound to traditional narratives, logical fallacies, and religious dogmas, Satanism can lead the way to free thinking, freedom from oppression, and new ways of being.

Through an objective view that seeks to free itself from the individual-self biases and dichotomies within, Satanism can win the hearts of the people. It challenges people to be free of own assumptions about gender, the perversion of false friendship, ridiculous dogma, the obscenity of good taste, and the offensive notion that we have to acquiesce to majority rule.

Works cited

A&E Television Networks. "Stonewall Riots." 31 May, 2017. *History*, 2 Nov. 2019, https://www.history.com/topics/gay-rights/the-stonewall-riots. Accessed 1 Sept. 2019.

ALA Literacy Clearinghouse. "Information Literacy." American Library Association, 2019, https://literacy.ala.org/information-literacy/. Accessed 1 Sept. 2019.

Bell, Matthew. "The US Just Officially Recognized the Satanic Temple as a Religion." *Business Insider*, 7 May, 2019, https://www.businessinsider.com/the-us-just-officially-recognized-the-satanic-temple-as-a-religion-2019-5. Accessed 1 Sept. 2019.

Chappell, Bill. "Arkansas Installs a New Ten Commandments Monument at its Capitol." *NPR*, 26 Apr. 2018 https://www.npr.org/sections/thetwo-way/2018/04/26/606029241/arkansas-installs-a-new-ten-commandments-monument-at-its-capitol/. Accessed 1 Sept. 2019.

Coll, Steve. "Donald Trump's 'Fake News' Tactics." *The New Yorker*, 3 Dec. 2017, https://www.newyorker.com/

magazine/2017/12/11/donald-trumps-fake-news-tactics. Accessed 1 Sept. 2019.

Goldberg, Susan. "Special Issue: Gender Revolution." *National Geographic*, Jan. 2017, https://www.nationalgeographic.com/pdf/gender-revolution-guide.pdf. Accessed 1 Sept. 2019.

Morgenstern, Joe. "'Hail Satan?' Review: What the Devil Are They After?" *Wall Street Journal*, 18 Apr. 2019, https://www.wsj.com/articles/hail-satan-review-what-the-devil-are-they-after-11555618948. Accessed 1 Sept. 2019.

Romano, Aja. "The History of Satanic Panic in the US—and Why it's not Over Yet." *Vox*, 30 Oct. 2016, https://www.vox.com/2016/0/30/13413864/satanic-panic-ritual-abuse-history-explained. Accessed 1 Sept. 2019.

Seminole State Library. "5 Components of Information Literacy." *Youtube*, 29 Jan. 2014, https://www.youtube.com/watch?v=1ronp6Iue9w. Accessed 1 Sept. 2019.

Shapiro, Ben. *Brainwashed: How Universities Indoctrinate America's Youth*. Thomas Nelson, 2010.

Smith, David. "'Enemy of the People': Trump's War on the Media is a Page from Nixon's Playbooks." *The Guardian*, 7 Sept. 2019, https://www.theguardian.com/us-news/2019/sep/07/donald-trump-war-on-the-media-oppo-research. Accessed 1 Sept. 2019.

The Satanic Temple. "What Does Satan Mean to TST?" Learn, https://thesatanictemple.com/pages/learn. Accessed 1 Sept. 2019.

Washington Post. "Anton S. Lavey Dies at 67." 9 Nov. 1997, https://www.washingtonpost.com/archive/local/1997/11/09/anton-s-lavey-dies-at-67/c546b323-acb9-463e-ad96-7da298f9e4d8/. Accessed 1 Sept. 2019.

Satanism's Brilliant Heart of Darkness: Duality of Spirit Transformed into a Singularity of Self

+

Kirsten Banger

I have a certain duality of spirit. Duality of mind, of self, of personality—however, it can be defined, or not defined. And, yes, I am aware that most people aren't just one thing. But, if you're a woman especially, you've been taught from birth that you are supposed to be exactly that. From your appearance to how you act, and think, and even how you speak—that's it. Game over. And so you walk around with this widening schism inside of you, and any minute now you feel like you're going to break apart in a million pieces. You fit, and yet you know you don't fit at the same time.

And so I put myself deliberately on the fringe of society when I was younger, defining my identity within the relative safety of counterculture movements like punk and goth. And there were fringe groups within the fringe groups. People who wanted to be vampires, the more serious and established BSDM culture, and those who toyed around with Satanism. Rather, a concept of Satanism that was more designed to horrify than anything I remembered reading in Anton LaVey's *The Satanic Bible* as a child.

These young practitioners actually did go out and cause harm to animals in some mistaken interpretation of Satanic rituals, and I lost whatever intellectual curiosity I might have had about Satanism. And yet, I too tried to conform to some mythical doctrine, to be as callous as the rest of society in regards to animals and nature; but, I was never part of the status quo.

Unfortunately, I don't remember as much as I should from *The Satanic Bible* back in the 80s, and am probably overdue for a reread. But I do remember that Satanism, as defined by Anton LaVey, also did not seem to have a place for women, especially not in the mind of a girl instinctually leaning towards feminism by trying to establish a sense of self in a world where every single thing was telling her not to be that self. I didn't need to be told another way to be, especially when I was already trying to fit in with the cool misfits of the 90s subculture scene. So, I floated into Neo-Paganism. It became a spiritual explanation for my oddball belief that animals and even plants and trees, were sentient; could feel pain, and deserved to be treated with the same respect as humans, if not more. And that it gave me an excuse to continue to be the sensitive, tree-hugging girl that fiercely loved, not just horses, but all animals. Oh yeah, and unicorns, and fairies and any other creature of mythical lore. And I dedicated myself to animal rights causes, as a real -life parallel.

And so, Satanism through this narrow lens, became unfortunately linked with the anti-women/ hyper-masculine practitioners that I came in contact with in the world outside of books. I admit it: from my young-woman perspective, they were not just some scary bogeymen as defined by traditional society and in movies; they were a real, hate-filled threat to me, and to many of my friends. I certainly didn't feel that I had a place in their society, however stereotypical (or actual) my perception of them was back then. I was still very much a child;

confused, lost, and trying to find a place in the world.

I am now entering into middle age. And, in some ways, I'm still that lost and confused girl, trying to find a place in the world. A world in which, shockingly, the threat for women is still omnipresent. Society has not become any safer for girls, young women, or even adult women in general. And that's where Satanism came in, surprisingly.

Neo-Paganism is all-well-and-good for fostering the imagination, but since I have allowed myself to become a writer, all of that has moved more and more into my inner world. I still feel connected to trees and animals and lovely insects, but I write about them. And I can keep unicorns and fairies and kelpies alive in my writing. That world feels just as real as my outer world and self.

I'm a pretty practical thinker. I like common-sense thinking—clarity of thought, and of course, science (except ineffectual experiments on animals). But I'm staunchly behind the science that proves that climate change, whether people want to believe it or not, is happening all around us. And it's destroying what I most love about this world.

And my pain, sadness, and anger is not unrealistic or overly sensitive or futile.

And then, right smack in the middle of this emotionally draining midlife crisis, I had to do some research into Satanism and the devil for a short story I was writing. During that research, I discovered new Satanic groups that fiercely support science and knowledge, rights for women, and children, and liberation from traditional societal decrees in general.

That's when I began looking deeper into Satanism. It's not about a mythological devil, who doesn't really exist, or evil, or even punishment for the evil in humanity. In my understanding, it's a tool, and one that's come along at a much-needed time in my own development. It states that the responsibility is ours. We screwed things up, and there's no divine higher power that's going to come down and fix things. Or extraterrestrials. Our sins are ours to actively atone for, not to accept passive forgiveness about, and we need to come together as a whole to do that, not only become a better version of humanity by our own standards, but to not let anyone detract from that, just because it's the way it's always been done.

Satanism symbolizes self-actualization. It represents empowerment, for better or for worse. For making mistakes but to keep on growing, keep on evolving. It is learning. Lucifer is the light-bringer, steeped in women-centric understanding and earthly co-operation, but the reality is that we have to learn to be light-bringers ourselves, and it's hard work. It's knowledge, not only about science, and the world, but learning about who we are. And learning from, like animals and their society, so that we can become better stewards of this planet—learn how to be part of this planet, not above it.

As a woman entering middle age, I'm getting more and more resistant to people dictating to me who I am, what I should think—what I should feel (or not feel)—such as doctors, who attempt to dictate to women what's "not allowed" to happen to their bodies—or their minds. No one gets to tell me that things that are happening to my physical body are just all in my head.

It's about recognizing that maybe I'm *evil* as well as *good* in the stereotypical sense, and that I make bad choices as a result. But accepting that it's part of me, and I'm not going to let anyone tell me how I should be. That it's really about my empowerment–that power comes from within me.

The tenets of Satanism then, lend credence to my growing confidence. More than that, they've helped me realize that I matter, I have a voice, and a personality, and that I need to be strong in that self, to trust my own natural evolution over what has been dictated to me my entire life. Satanism, in this transition to middle age, is liberation. I have allied myself with certain Satanist credos to not only liberate myself, but to share in that symbolic and timely liberation with others.

That belief comes from the fact that it's the twenty-first century, and it's time to let go of a society that is largely restrictive, anti-democratic, conformist, oppressive, and, therefore, move into a new interpretation of humanity that doesn't rely on archaic definitions of humanity's so-called natural state that often operates against nature. We are part of nature. Whether humanity accepts it or not, I, for one, will not continue to be silenced by the established order.

Satanism doesn't have all the answers, but I don't have to believe it does. I have to believe in me, and not waste time and energy in judging myself, or even others. I'm not going to be smote down by some angry deity if I grow past its credos; Satan is symbolic in my acceptance of it as a religious practice. So, for now, Satanism is a doorway to a new way of thinking, and to direct action via personal responsibility, and my dual selves think that's just fine.

Better to Reign, to Reign Ourselves Better: Satanism in the 21st Century

✠

Charles N. Bernard

What is Satanism, and who are Satanists? What values do they espouse, and what paths led them to identify with a mythical figure who is traditionally portrayed as the embodiment of sin and immorality? I suspect that were you to ask a dozen Satanists, you would get a dozen widely disparate answers. Satanism, after all, emphasizes free thinking and encourages the asking of questions and the pursuit of individual inquiry more than any other religious philosophy. Still, these disparate answers would have common themes. Many of us started our journey in a traditional and conservative religious milieu. Many experienced a loss of faith (or an acknowledgement that we never had it to begin with), which either was preceded by or followed from the asking of factual and philosophical questions that placed the insufficiency of our given religion into sharp relief—a relief that it severed the mental shackles that kept us in thrall to the idea of deity.

Satanism exists in part as a reaction to monotheistic faiths. Given the theological and narrative ecosystem of the United States—the stories that are told, the assumptions that undergird social interactions, the images and concepts we absorb throughout our moral development—the emergence of a philosophy aligned with the figure of Satan is natural, even inevitable. Satanism is the inheritor of some of monotheism's symbolism, a reclamation of humanity from the imaginary claws of the angels. The grip of those claws is fierce: though statistical data tells us that participation in traditional religion has declined, the hard core of zealots and dominionists that remain have ratcheted up their attempts to gain and cement political power, imposing their vision of hierarchy, puritanical "morality," and regressive social structures on the rest of us.

As this struggle unfolds in the United States, from Alabama to Zion, it's worth asking why adherence to traditional religion is on the decline. The causes are numerous. First, abuse in religious communities is rampant as seen with the example within the Catholic church, where the only horror equal to the revelations of widespread child sex abuse were revelations of a systematic and deliberate cover-up of same. As places where children are taught submission and obedience and leaders are seen as literal intercessors with the divine (stand-ins for the Almighty, if you will), religious communities are vulnerable to predation, and in many cases unwilling to grapple with that fact.

Another likely contributor to the decline of religious commitment is the broad decline of social capital in America over the last century: the decay of generalized networks of trust and reciprocity that help build strong neighborhoods and vibrant cities and towns (this decline is traced expertly by Dr. Robert Putnam in his two landmark books, *Bowling Alone* and *Better Together*). Add to that the steady advance of science and technology in answering questions about the origins of humanity and our place in the universe—answers that have forced the retreat of religion's claims to truth and validity—and it's easy to see that the theistic establishment is facing headwinds unprecedented in recent memory.

Many religious communities that have weathered these changes and thus survived into 2019 share certain characteristics, most of them negative in nature, but a few beneficial. Regarding the beneficial, religious traditions today primarily serve the same purpose that religion has since the dawn of humanity: assuaging (or at least sublimating) the existential terror produced by the foreknowledge of our mortality.

Religious doctrines attempt to convey ethical principles as well, albeit principles that in some cases are corroded, inverted, and counterproductive. Communities of worship can also promote fellowship and provide support during personal difficulty, and, perhaps most importantly of all, religion provides a narrative—something that humans need. We need a narrative because the world is vast, more vast than can possibly be accommodated by a one-to-one representation in our minds, no matter how scientific our worldview.

In his masterful short story "On Exactitude in Science," Jorge Luis Borges gives an allegory of the map-territory relation in which an empire, famous for cartography, creates the ultimate map, one in which everything is represented perfectly at one-to-one scale. The ensuing map is, of course, the size of the territory it is meant to represent, and is thus useless. The map winds up discarded. I take Borges' story to mean that we need maps because they hold more information than we can carry in our minds alone. They help us navigate the world. Maps, by their nature, must be simplified representations so that we can use them. So, it is the same with narratives: they provide a map of the world, and thus use symbols and allegory to simplify very complex sets of ideas so that we can, metaphorically, take them with us.

Praise should be given where it's due. Some religious communities provide maps of reality that, while they elevate the "divine" and cater to the "soul" more than human potential, do promote ideals that Satanists share. Compassion, empathy, justice for marginalized communities—these can be found within American religious communities of virtually all kinds. Examples include he third pillar of Islam, zakat, or charitable giving. Catholic Community Services is one of the largest refugee resettlement agencies in the world. The civil rights movement that struck down legal segregation and Jim Crow grew and thrived thanks to black Christian churches. Judaism in the US has a rich history of not just charitable organization and donation, but contributions to the emancipation of other minority groups. In all of these cases the narratives—the maps—are what religion gave humans, which has led to selfless and empathic behavior. Even if it comes from a desire to serve the divine rather than a more direct wish to help our fellow beings, this is to be acknowledged and applauded.

The maps of reality that traditional religions have provided are poorly suited to the world in which we live as of 2019. Traditional, social, and political reactionary religions view humanity as steeped in sin, essentially unworthy, or at least worthy only of suffering—supposedly in the name of purification. This strain of religious inclination is built on faith and belief in things impossible and unprovable, or, in many embarrassing cases, scientifically disproven. Buried even deeper than the miracles, though, is the foundational idea of submission and supplication, ethereally to a Divine Dictator, but terrestrially to "His" duly appointed minions. Humanity has often been badgered by these holy men (almost always men) whose immaculate example of obedience to celestial dictates we are told to strive to emulate. Sometimes we are even told of god-men or god-kings, the very existence of which as a category should fill anyone who truly values reason, freedom, and equality with nausea. The concept of a cosmic sovereign belongs to the same bloodstained reliquary of history as the divine right of kings. Love of and devotion to unchecked power is a sickness that has been allowed to plague the world for too long, and, when you get right down to it, divinity represents the ultimate expression of unaccountable and arbitrary authority.

"Fair enough," one might say. "But why 'Satanism?' Why not 'atheism,' or 'humanism?'"

A fair question with a simple answer. Both atheism and humanism are perfectly fine terms, but they fall short in a few crucial ways. Before we go any further, we ought to define a few terms. "Atheism" refers to the lack of belief in a supernatural deity or deities, and "humanism" to a system of thought that emphasizes potential human value, goodness, and commonality, and seeks a rational solution to human problems.

These are my definitions of (with a devilish wink at C.S. Lewis) "mere" atheism and "mere" humanism, but they are "mere" in the truest definition of the word as well: solely and no more than is specified. Mere atheism is a lack of belief in deities; it provides no positive ideology, understood solely by itself. One can, for example, be an atheist and profess either firebrand Marxism or Ayn-Randian Objectivism, and you would be hard-pressed to find two ideologies with more diametrically opposed value systems. Mere humanism is defined by a more discrete set of ideas that revolve around a positive view of human potential and seek to emphasize common human needs and solutions that meet said needs. Humanism in and of itself does not provide certain things that contribute enormously to human well-being: fellowship, ritual, symbolism, and a narrative or narratives.

Not all narratives are created equal. Both the concept of original sin and the concept of hell are terrible things to inflict upon a child during moral and intellectual development—or upon anyone else, for that matter. Telling people that they are intrinsically evil, that they are "fallen" and thus consigned to unending and unimaginable torture after death is an act of almost incomprehensible sadism and aggression; to what end do parents and Sunday school teachers hurt young children this way? Ostensibly, to instill an ethical code of conduct that will make them better people. But a synthesis of current research on the subject shows no clear correlation between religion and altruism (Saroglou 439-457, Skitka). And all of that is assuming that the abuses children are subject to are limited to the intended variety, and don't include sexual exploitation by an adult—a crime which, with each passing year, more religious faiths are revealed to have covered up and thus been party to.

So, if hell and original sin have questionable utility as spurs to ethical behavior what purpose do they serve? There are two explanations, one theological and one practical. Theologically, original sin allows monotheists to square the circle of omnibenevolence and omnipotence with a deity that is the supposed embodiment of all that is good allow children to starve to death, or good people to suffer horrible calamities?

Humanity's earliest attempts at religious worldviews featured deities who were human-like—given to passions and errors—and who constituted a sort of squabbling divine aristocracy more than a universal monarchy (Holland, "The Gods of Syria-Palestine"). In this context, misfortune and ill in the world made sense. As religious culture in Mesopotamia shifted from polytheism to henotheism (worshiping one god while acknowledging the existence of others, as with the early roots of Judaism) to monotheism, original sin entered the equation as a reason that an all-powerful, all-good deity would allow suffering. The narrative shifted to, "God loves us perfectly, but we love Him imperfectly." The concept of hell (for those who believed or believe it) comes from a similar source: the lack of earthly justice evidenced by predation and inequality is a temporary state of affairs, this postmortem judgment suggests (Holland, "The Problem of Evil") .Those you hate, either because they have wronged you or because you find them frightening or immoral, will get what is coming to them eventually.

In a practical sense, it could be said that the concepts of original sin and hell, of an apocalyptic judgment to come and a Heavenly Father who knows best, have done a great deal to prop up society's priestly class and possessors of wealth and power, and have hindered the progress of humanity toward a more equitable state of affairs. Additionally, these narratives—these myths that we tell ourselves and each other, that undergird a great deal of modern American culture—can prevent people from taking this world as seriously as they should. Why work to end hunger, if a table is prepared in heaven? Why strive to be better, if you are simultaneously a moral failure from birth and at the same time already washed and absolved of all your crimes by proxy? This illogic all stems from the fact that "sin" is best understood as behavior or thought that is unethical because it is "against god."

This fixes the center of ethical behavior in regard for the preferences of an invisible and highly uncommunicative despot, rather than in regard for our fellow beings and the world in which we all live. Unethical or selfish human behavior can be accurately understood and addressed as occurring in the context of mundane humanity, of psychology and social forces rather than the fluctuations of divine mystery. "Sin" is meaningless unless you accept "god." Those of us who are proudly godless believe that actions that harm others are crimes against those others, not against a deity, and thus to make things right, retribution must be terrestrial, not celestial. If I do wrong, my ethical responsibility belongs to this world, to my fellow living beings. I do not accept that I was born carrying some cosmic bar tab, especially not a cosmic bar tab that someone else is going to pay or has paid on my behalf. We must all settle our own debts when it comes to our actions. That's not to say that context and mercy shouldn't be integral parts of our concept of justice, but it's not the responsibility of another to make recompense on my or anyone else's behalf.

In the 21st century, we need a religious philosophy that rejects the darkness of the past, and seeks to illuminate the future. Satanism is a system of ethics established without the pretense of divinity—by and for humans. It is a force for good, and against gods. It is a religion, but an atheistic one. It celebrates Satan as a symbol of rebellion against arbitrary authority, but makes no claim of a supernatural or personal Satan. Indeed, given that Satanism recognizes no actual god, recognizing an actual devil would not make a great deal of sense. Both a celebration of individual liberty and an invitation to solidarity, Satanism does not despise the flesh or fixate on cleansing some ethereal "soul." I am a product of my flesh just as my flesh is a product of entirely natural (and comprehensible) processes.

Humanity is no miracle, "created" separate from—and superior to—the rest of "creation." Each of us is one link in a chain that stretches back billions of years, a connection and a history forged within our very DNA.

Much of the history of "evil" is comprised of attempts, on the part of the "good," to restrict behavior that harms no one, but of which is disapproved. These restrictions have often been on sexual behavior; specifically, in many cases, the sexual behavior of women. Satanism emphasizes the paramount importance and central role of enthusiastic consent, and beyond that, celebrates the right of individuals to love whomever they choose, without the interference of religious potentates. Each person's body belongs only to them, not to "god" or those who claim to speak on behalf of the divine. Love, joy, human connection: these are the gifts given us by our DNA, the fruition of our development as a species and a human community, and should be celebrated.

This emphasis on compassion and empathy, and on the common things that unite us as all, is an element of humanism that has been missing from previous iterations of Satanism. While it is true that selfishness is not a sin inasmuch as "sin" is a meaningless concept, and inasmuch as we should love ourselves and treat ourselves with kindness, excessive selfishness is a maladaptive trait—one that indicates incomplete moral development. Recognizing ourselves in others and others in ourselves has nothing whatsoever to do with gods or messiahs; it is part of our proud heritage as great apes, cousins to other tool-makers, shrine-builders, and learners of language. Satanism in the 21st century teaches empathy and compassion alongside the values of freethinkers whom have come before.

Compassion. Justice. Empathy. A belief in freedom. These are central values to Satanism, and are also values currently being weighed and tested by the legal system in the United States. Liberation is an eternally ongoing struggle that has been pursued by people of many identities, separated by race, class, gender, and sexual identity, but always united, in one way or another, around the idea that our bodies are inviolable, subject to our wills alone. Satan is a symbol of rebellion, the eternal cry of "non serviam" (I will not serve) to all tyrants. As reactionary and retrograde social movements grasp for power in the United States, and as similar groups continue to gain ground in places ranging from Brazil to Britain to Bethlehem, the world needs Satanism, needs freethinkers, and heretics, and people willing to interrogate power.

So, it is that I celebrate human potential; celebrate the ideals of freedom, compassion, and justice—in appreciation of my own emancipation from gods and anti-human, anti-reality ideologies—say, "Hail Satan!"

Works Cited

Holland, Glenn S. "Religion in the Ancient Mediterranean World: The Gods of Syria-Palestine." *The Great Courses*, https://www.thegreatcourses.com/courses/religion-in-the-ancient-mediterranean-world.html. Accessed 21 Sept. 2019.

--. "Religion in the Ancient Mediterranean World: Syria-Palestine—The Problem of Evil." *The Great Courses,* https:/www.thegreatcourses.com/courses/religion-in-the-ancient-mediterranean-world.html. Accessed 21 Sept. 2019.

Saroglou, V. "Religion, Spirituality, and Altruism." In K. I. Pargament et al. (Eds.). *APA handbook of Psychology, Religion, and Spirituality: Context, Theory, and Research*, vol 1. American Psychological Association, 2013, http://dx.doi.org/10.1037/14045-024

Skitka Linda J. et al. (2018) "Moral and Religious Convictions: Are They the Same or Different Things?" *Plos One*, vol. 13, no. 6. https://doi.org/10.1371/journal.pone.0199311

References

Putnam, Robert *Better Together*. New York, Simon & Schuster, 2003.

--. *Bowling Alone*. New York, Simon & Schuster, 2000.

PART 2

CREATIVE NONFICTION

[Rā'Dē—əM] GIRLS

+

JANINE MERCER

I

I raise the brush to my lips and twirl it slightly, bringing the hair of the bristles to a fine point. Lick. Dip. Tip. I am one of many, crowded into a small grey room lined with long tables. Around me, women accept dials from thin metal trays as if selecting fare from the dessert tray at a fine restaurant. They are wearing white gloves to prevent fingerprints when lifting the faces from their packing crates. My fingers, spotted and smeared with dried UnDark, get the opportunity to select a delicacy. In 1902, William J. Hammer brought radium salt to the United States in his trouser pocket, blissfully unaware of the harm it might cause, thinking instead of the bulge soon to be occupying his wallet. The resulting mark on his upper thigh from contact with the substance left Hammer puzzled, but he thought little of it. It was not of concern. When blended with zinc oxide and a little glue, the resulting paint could be used to illuminate watch faces, switch plates, gun sights, and also cause human bone to glow through flesh in complete darkness. I delicately lift twelve dials from the tray by their edges, in various sizes, setting them down next to several others. Lick. Dip. Tip. I am commended on my performance and speed, a whore to the process. I do not feel my life slowly slipping away from me. I do not feel my bones absorb that which would make a Geiger counter weep. I do not see my body give out a steady light without flame as others do as if observing a gelatinous jellyfish lying prone on the sand calling to a potential mate with its bioluminescence. They contain a unique compound called luciferin. When exposed to oxygen, a chemical reaction aided along by an enzyme called luciferase emits light. The natural light my body emits is 1000 times too weak for the human eye to perceive but, with the aid of Lucifer himself, the invisible becomes visible. Lick. Dip. Tip. Out of the corner of my eye, I see another painter using the radium as eyeshadow. It's good for you. Or so they say.

Radium Girls

II

Dollar signs flash in the yellow of their eyes as our bones become brittle, honeycomb without the presence of bees. Wolves, in the heat of pack mentality, will devour every chicken in the henhouse. Fine neck bones will snap and blood will flash black against the barn wood in the twilight hours. Bones will lay stripped, pale, glowing. These morning hours, the twilight, is UnDark. In the UnDark, we all glow. We are all effervescent. They tell us the amount of product we're working with is utterly harmless, it is ridiculous to even suggest. The pack watches from just beyond the door, through a window, arms folded, smiles curling their lips, not realizing that they too are being enveloped by the UnDark, that their bones are becoming spongy, that soon they will remove fractured fragments from their jaws without anesthetic. That the pieces will slip through flesh, now mottled black, and appear in their hands in the most forlorn act of prestidigitation. In a back room, shipping containers piled high, men tasked with unloading the radium from trucks are issued heavy leaded aprons and thick gloves. In their hunger and their ignorance, they too are prey. I will not be the only one eaten by the UnDark. They too will become meat for a beast far larger. Completely flavorless, the only side effect of ingesting radium is rosy cheeks. Years later, I will attend their funerals, stand idly by their tombstones with my eyes downcast because the natural light is something I cannot bear. Blindness and a failing of my balance will prevent me from laying a flower on the casket. It will prevent me from sifting a handful of dirt, ashes to ashes, through my delicate fingers, bones now unbearably thin. I will not cry for you. You who told me to put the brush in my mouth. You who leered at me through the glass. I am the face of radium in the way that some women smile for the camera, giving a cheeky smile as they dip to reveal the supple mounds of their bosom, proffering a bottle of perfume.

III

Tho-Radia du docteur Alfred Curie, essence de radium pur maintenant en poudre et en crème. Un produit pour améliorer votre teint qui laisse une peau lisse et sans imperfections. Redonnez à votre peau son éclat de jeunesse! Une famille de produits qui rend les lèvres saines et les joues roses à tomber. Curie's fine products. Lipsticks and blushes, blemish creams and powders, that will create a look to die for. Your man will be enthralled!

In shop windows, a woman with porcelain skin stares out at onlookers, blonde locks curled perfectly, lips in a subtle pout. Made more beautiful by radium. If you tapped a finger gently on her vixen face, would the porcelain chip like the delicate rim of a fine china teacup? Face lifting without surgery. SELL Radium Princess Lingerie! "I want to pay you $85/wk. Man or woman." Profits in advance! The element was hailed as a panacea for everything from blindness to hysteria. The ad's raved, "No medicine, no drugs. Just a light, small, comfortable, inexpensive Radio-Active Pad worn on the back by day and over the stomach at night." Feeling sporty but want to protect the family jewels? "The Radiendocinator can be worn like any athletic strap and is easy and comfortable to use!" The inventor was also a frequent user of his creation, but not for very long. A short time later, he died of bladder cancer. "Revigator! The perpetual health spring of Radium Water is proving a revelation of new health and vitality to some of Seattle's most prominent musicians! Revigator means NEW LIFE!" In the 20th century, the only way to make butter healthier was to name it after radium. Radithor is "liquid sunshine" that is good and good for you, invigorating and will add a bounce to your step. After you lose most of your jaw, it will bounce you all the way into your lead-lined coffin in Pittsburg. The headlines read, "DEATH OF MOST FAMOUS CONSUMER" even though ten women had died from the "occupational illness" four years prior. Astringent contre les bactéries. Stérilisez vos cavités et prévenez la gingivite! Masser les dents et les gencives et avoir une bouche en bonne santé. Blanchir l'intégrité de la dentition! That's all fine and good, until you can pull your teeth out by hand. At least they'll be white.

IV

The clouds are cumulus, laying typically just below 6,500 feet in the azure blue. I read about clouds in the third grade and did my science fair project on cloud formations. I learned to draw them early on in grade school. When I was four and my father asked me to draw clouds, I drew cumulus clouds. Like snowflakes symbolize winter, cumulus clouds are stand-ins for every "draw a cloud" situation. Cumulonimbus clouds, the kind that looks solid and resembles the cotton batting layer from couch backs, were here yesterday knocking on my window and shaking their fists, threatening rain. They bring the storm, but the storm was already here. This morning, as I brushed my teeth, my jaw felt strange. At the periphery of my vision, I could see the UnDark creeping closer. I slipped my fingers into my mouth, probing along the bases of my bottom teeth with shaking fingertips until I found it. A hole, about the size of a pencil eraser, and then a small pointed object slightly offset, askew. An adverb usually reserved to describe the wearing of a hat, the hanging of a piece of art. Askew. Out of line. Used as comedy. Harry fell backward over the ottoman, his glasses askew, and we all chuckled gayly. The dentist says it's part of the mental foramen. It's been slipping around hidden just under the soft flesh of my palate for at least a month. An ulcer has formed around the mental protuberance, an effort by my body to contain the foreign object. Not foreign. It was once a part of me. I am taking it on the chin. A phrase that originated in boxing implying a straight or critical punch. An uppercut. Taking it on the chin. Stand up for yourself. Don't complain. Get on with it. Today, as a stand in the lawyer's office, shifting my weight from one foot to another to alleviate the stress on my hip bones, I perform minor surgery as invisibly as I can. I gingerly pull the piece of bone from the hole and extract it. There is no pain. I gingerly place the object in a handkerchief, fold it twice, and slip it into my purse. There are no scalpels. There is no anesthetic. The lawyer says that I am afflicted with an occupational illness. I must fight for compensation. My lawyer says U.S. Radium Corp. knew how dangerous UnDark was, telling its company chemists to wear leaded aprons and create safe handling pamphlets for its employees. They wanted their people to work safely. They wanted their people to live, to have children and collect social security. I am taking it on the chin. Get on with it.

PART 3

POETRY

UP—RISING

+

CHANGMING YUAN

Unable to endure constant burning
the suffering Satans finally find their ways
from hell through the topsoil, trying
to rise together
with the summer sun.

Yet they are all shot
with its very first needles
into the darkest moment of last night
where the ghosts of the newly dead, the invisible
linger on, staring at one another.

No one knows how many of them
were still holding their authentic
human shapes, how many of them
became deformed, agonizing—
pools of stinking blood

and piles of rotten flesh.

A Lust Letter from Lucifer to Judas

+

Misako Yamazaki

For Judas—the only human I've ever loved

You'll be back
with your dry lips
and honey-coated tongue—
resting in your mouth
like a sinner on Sunday morning.

I love you, Judas.
I love your Nile river veins
and the mountain ridges on your back.
I want to run my fingers
and split tongue over them,
taste the salt and sweat
and humanity on your skin.
You are everything but the sunrise to me.
I'll get tangled in your hair like the branches
of the tree you hanged yourself from;

A Lust Letter From Lucifer

I'll bite your neck like a vampire
until you melt in my bed.
I want to find your sweet spot again.
I want to find you.

Your eyes burn
like hot coals
with the thought of everything you've ever wanted.

I'll love you like an animal—wild,
like how you know you need.

I want to rip you out
from the dirt your mother buried you in,
and hum against your lips, down here,
where it's colder than kelvin until you hum back to life.

I'll water your filthy roots with my sinful touch.

When you come back to me,
bring your demons on their leashes;
I'll tame them for you
like I've tamed you—
wrap yourself in my skin,
keep yourself cold.

-»

I'll make sure you live forever, next to me—
against me.
We'll make our own mythology and rewrite the Bible—the history—
the whole goddamn universe.

If you decide you don't prefer the eternal cold after all,
I'll press my hands to yours and warm you up.
Your breath will fog up between us
and I'll breathe it in like cigarette smoke.
We'll move together,
make fault lines on each other—tectonic plates,
cracking my tables and chairs—
my living room floor.
I'll make oceans in your name; god isn't the only one with power here.

We're two lonely souls but fuck, Judas,
you'll come back to me.
You'll come home—my prodigal lover.
You'll come back,
and when you knock on my door
I'll let you in

A Lust Letter From Lucifer

I will wash your feet
and the guilt
and the fear...and the loneliness with my tears.

I will be your light, your morning star;
I'll put a crown of leucadendrons on your head
and we'll laugh and be happy—finally.

Judas.

Baby, when you come back home, we'll fall to-
gether as hard and fast as you want.
I know you always crave my fallen angel love.
I know you crave it too.

We both know you've never been good at being sober.

You're gonna come back to me, Judas,
everyone always does.
I'm like an addictive rollercoaster ride
always the same and everyone knows it;
so goddamn good I never go out of business.
They crave the high, the adrenaline rush, the cli-
max and post-coital bliss.

→»

We'll forgive each other,
and our bodies will be scorching when they touch.

We'll make a fireplace out of hell;
no more chattering teeth,
only rumpled bed sheets and honey whiskey—
just you and me.

D.O.A.—DAWN OF AGRICULTURE

+

MARK BUCKLEY

Before the Dawn Of Agriculture men like ME where slapped into the shadow of sexual shame but now who needs muscles or chiseled chins, great size or strength, a lover's passion or a manly countenance 'cause for ten thousand years now I can persecute any female for infidelity towards ME and hold paternity privilege over MY biological children because we exceptional farmers invented marriage to destroy human sexuality by enslaving women with MY property for sex so I no longer need to share or compete or settle for an alpha males' sloppy seconds within foraging groups that are forced to share what they carry with them instead of our enforced legal couplings that takes the innocent, primal pleasure and mystery out of sex by connecting shtupping to birth thanks to dirt MY dirt MY very own thousand acres of seeded soil littered with pens full of MY trapped sheep, cattle, goats and pigs which means I can pork any female I fancy and destroy any man who thwarts MY desire as simply as the bulls I castrate into submission to easily herd into MY slaughterhouses that feed all the inferior people no longer dependent on their hunting and gathering skills but on ME to stay alive so not only am I not considered a sociopath by hoarding food but am praised at harvest time like a goddamned Babe Ruth hero because I have legally claimed and legally raped those precious few life-giving inches of topsoil with rotating crops and extended grasslands that exhausts and shrinks the earth, MY earth MY reign of forcing agricultural workers to bend over in the fields, stupidly exposing hairless backs to sun poisoning instead of their protective hunters' heads of hair harvesting MY food that shrinks the testicles of everyone who is forced to feed on the cheap calories of MY industrialized plants and animals that lowers fertility, but who needs big balls anymore when you don't have to kill larger animals in order to survive or attract females with your superior physical attributes proving I am the social parasite Sultan of Swat who grows fat on the food I've seized by stealing public land in the name of government protected ownership as the leader of a vicious pack of hyenas circling a luscious, lovely lamb like you because I am your superior and you know it despite your jealousy of my factory farm fresh endowments and of my lavish, decadent life-style that turns the lips on your face and the lips between your legs moist with desire as you ache to suckle my vegetable love that grows bigger, thick-er, stronger than any inferior substitute you can pluck from wild dark forests you pretend contain freedom from want but what I want I get and what I get I need and I want I need is for you to fall to your knees in phallic worship of my industrial con-tainer that turns my package into the most sought after edible on God's green earth so hail to thee oh Dawn of Agriculture the holy D.O.A!

Satan Calls You

Mark Andrew Heatcote

A Cobra whispers to a Horned Lizard
"He's got a-good-foothold on ears and minds."
They're lining up tens of millions adrift.
Satan profits from each of the four winds
Our sense of injustice-isn't-rectified
He afflicts and conflicts our flesh, assists
In a manner meaningful, quantified
People, never ask…does Satan exists?
His adversary, questionable
Did you read the memo, "Prayer is dead?"
…That dude-Lucifer the unmentionable
Caused the death of Catholicism; discs of bread,
Warm wine represents the blood of Christ body.
People love their abyss of drugs and drink
They don't whine-on about melancholy,
Bodied in a hot daisy-chain interlink-
They're all happy wayfaring Infidels.
Who'd give up rosemary-beads and sandals?
For scenes from the bowels of hells brothels
For lascivious moments, hot scandals

SATAN CALLS YOU

Lives become somewhat tainted with neglect
Folks sleeping-rough on every city-street
Of their fate, that political, excrete…
No-longer care, who is the architect
That's ejaculated, in every, tabloid
Tells us it's a dog eat dog world, stays guarded
Closed, captured black and white in celluloid;
Live life in-full-Technicolor, uncharted.
Have your sexual mishaps let them shape you
Desire is the clay, vessel that reshapes you
So slip-on as many shoes as you dare too
Be diverse, explore another avenue.

The Masses

+

Matthew Skaggs

It's not loud enough
I'm not drunk enough
I'm not high enough
I can still hear Him call

Run run run like you mean it
change change change like you mean it

My friends are all fools
they should ignore it like I do
when life calls on me
I just turn on the TV

Pray pray pray like you mean it
Fade fade fade like you mean it

I'm not broke enough
I'm not loved enough
I'm not meek enough
to stop this addiction

The Masses

Take take take like you mean it
hate hate hate like you mean it

friends are all fools
breaking all the rules
allow that to continue
making me miserable

Run run run like you mean it
pray pray pray like you mean it

I'm not rich enough
I'm not woke enough
I'm not smart enough
to be this cynical.

My Shadow

✢

Anthony Carias

I don't know what's wrong
but I do know something is up.
Sleeping has become bliss
forgetting my go to fix.

I even find it hard
to put my soul into words.
The closest I can describe
"me at the bottom of a puddle—
peaceful, drowning."

I'm patient, waiting
for a shark to swallow me whole,
or a hand to reach in and save my soul.
But they both always fail. As I wait, my skin
becomes pale.

My Shadow

And so, I'm stuck, drowning in a metaphor,
trying hard not to try anymore.
Letting all air escape me, reaching for it
I ask, what made me?

was it the stardust in my lungs
or the poison I injected into my brain?
was it destiny or I
that caused me to acknowledge pain
and why did I pick up a pen
thinking it would save me
as if I could write away
what's meant to stay

a part of me beyond control
please pardon me
it demands a toll—
it's come for the rest of my soul.

THE GREATEST TRICK

+

J. BARRETT WOLF

She opens her eyes
to the cell phone's alarm.
Somewhere there is a morning
that's not painted dull orange.

Coffee is the stimulant
of the masses. She drinks.
There is work at the end
of the same ride every day.

Work, where little is good,
nothing is better.
Where bosses boss as if
she were property.

Far away, there is war.
war is bad, they tell her—
"Do your job" or the terrorists win.
they know what is good—
For her, outside a barred window

marchers name fear and hate as virtues,
with colored signs and slogans,
they exalt the masters to protect them.

She is confused by the words,
arguments that sound right,
the failure of truth to conquer
a towering Babel of opinion.

They want to be safe,
to be comfortable in
their fortress homes
untroubled by fear.

On her way home
she sees a flash,
hears no thunder,
the sky blooms white.

DIGNITY INVERTED

+

THURSDAY SIMPSON

PART 1

THE AIR SMELLS LIKE BLOOD TODAY

My shit also smelled
of iron.

I've taken to
making pots
of coffee
with banana
or cherry
syrup.

I was about to
fall asleep,
but my bangs
started falling
forward.
A bad metaphorical
segway for

memories
of ex boyfriends
misgendering me
on purpose.

I can't make fuckall
of Deleuze
or Irigaray,

but I would gladly
accept a snail
trail
across my forward
or just a cock
to suck.

The saddest words in the
English language
are not goodbye,
but instead,
"Maybe some other
Time."

-»

PART 2

I NEVER FELT AT HOME UNTIL I MET PEOPLE

Who Hate Quentin Tarantino's Films
as much as I do

Citing *Clerks 2*,
my highschool
friends told
me licking someone's
asshole is a mistake.

When I was fifteen, the drummer
in my band and I
would stay up
all night playing
Dynasty Warriors
On the
PS2.

He introduced me to
Aqua Teen
Hunger Force
and was the
first boy

I knew
whom had
sex with
other
boys.

But he also
showed me
Kill Bill and when
I hated it,
we stopped being
friends.

I was alone
In a theater
with other
band mates
A few years
later when afterwards
everyone started
saying,
"Nat-see."

-»

During the 2008
election, they
all voted
for Ron Paul
or Mike
Huckabee.

None of them
ever once mentioned
Fred Williamson,
Bruce Lee, Dario Argento
or Robert Rodriguez.

PART 3
DIGITAL RAINBOWS

People talk so much
about ritual.

Satan as
Edgelord.

Joe Biden as
decent.
Joe Biden and
Eric Cartman

are avatars of the same
Incel Janus.
Everyone is a mobster until
they get a VHS tape of
their daughter
getting raped.

But perhaps
fantasy is a path
towards health.

A few years ago
a partner
told me
my self
control made
her sad.

It broke her
heart that I never
came undone,
could never fully
show myself
to someone
else.

→»

Growing up my family couldn't afford
childcare and my
parents were
always at
work.

So, after school
I stayed at some old woman's
house that got her
hair done at my
Mom's salon.

I watched a lot
of *Muppet Babies*
cartoons and learned
how to be
alone.

The Jedi are not
that different
from Roman
Catholics.
Everyone sides with
Obi Wan over
Anakin.

Everyone hates
Hayden Christensen,
everyone is so quick to
laugh when Anakin
says Obi Wan
turned Padme
against him.

Forced celibacy
also does bad things
to children.

Amanda Palmer criticizes
Lady Gaga and
Lana Del Rey,

everyone wants
a production
and quantifiable
examples of
Talent.

For a change,
I tried domming.
I met up with a

-»

new friend,
I tried to enjoy
hitting her

But couldn't resist
spending the night
sucking on her
cock, ruining
her orgasm denial
fantasy.

I think my newest fetish
is getting
ganged banged
by a group
of TERFS,

them calling me a
faggot while
they refuse to
let me taste
their pussies.
Sometimes the best
thing you can do
is listen to Ke$ha, drink too

much caffeine,

and jerk off
to the videos
of your ex
fucking her new boy-dom
and then go on
Tinder and
find a new
crush.

I love spitting up
brown phlegm every
morning in the shower, but
I don’t smoke,
so the coffee stains
mixed with blood
drawn from
my gums with my
new tooth
brush will
have to
do—

-»

repetition is
how I make
sense of
myself.

In 2008 I wanted to be a poet,
so in 2009
I brought a bottle of
Pink Catawba
and a copy of
Prince of
Darkness to
a party.

Some friends of
mine had
a threesome,

I walked out
into the woods
with a girl
I liked.
A tree had fallen
across
a gap over

the Iowa
River,
We climbed
out onto it
and I sang
something
I wrote
about her.

Occultists
and Rockabilly Queens
don't have to grow
up.

PART 4

I'LL SEE YOU IN THE DEVRON SYSTEM

The first time
I heard of
Star Trek,

my grandmother
bought me a
Commander La Forge
doll for
Christmas.

-»

She and I have the same disease,
we're women who
love to fuck.

Other than Holidays,
she was permanently
institutionalized.

I wanted to watch
The Next Generation
from start to
finish,
but didn't
have the
money for the
DVD's,
so instead
I skipped a lot of
school and tried to find
episodes of TNG
on cable television.
Something about the show
felt evil,

evil in the way the words
“eating out” sound so
delicious.

The girl from the woods
disappeared in a different
set of woods a
year later.

My next partner
whispered passages from Karl Ove
into my ears while we fucked.

I offered them the chance
to line two hooks through
my shoulders but
they decided
I was sick.

A few years later,
a different lover kept me around
after I licked up her squirt,
another broke up with me,

-»

immediately after asking
if she was
capable of squirting,

blaming pornography
and the way it ruins
us.

All of the working-class guys
I fucked during community
college are still
in the closet, married
and with children.

Sometimes I still think
about their endless variations of,
"Poetry won't get you laid,
poetry is for fags,
Iowa City is where the fags
live," I heard
when I told them my
plans for the future.

DIGNITY INVERTED

So many memories of
Kristeva boyfriends
at U Iowa
saying Satanism
is not authentic
theology,

endless variations of
Kristeva girlfriends
saying professional
wrestling is not
art.

When I was six years old,
I talked my grandmother
out of a psychotic break for
the first time.

I've always been good at keeping
people alive,

except for the times
I'm not.

-»

She died on the 4th of July, 2013.
A month later, I decided I'd
better watch the full series
of TNG before I myself
died.

Obviously I finished on the
4th of July a few years
after.

I wrote a long Facebook post
about being so humbled,
so grateful.

My first book about to be
published,

my work about to be anthologized by
Ariel Gore and Tiffany Scandal.

I wrote about how I always
preferred spending time
with my grandmother
in the hospital because
she and the other patients

gave me money and candy they
hid away for me
during the week.

Everywhere else,
people just called me spoiled,
a brat.

In a comment, one of my friends that
helped me transition
told me to go fuck
myself with my self
indulgence.

Such is life.

It seems so long ago,
staying up all night
in my dorm,
reading 600 pages of
War and Peace and then
half of *Crime and Punishment* a few
weeks later.

There are so many
people I miss.

For lack of a better
myth,

someday, I'll see you all
in the Devron system.

DUST

+

SHANNORA HENDRIX

She ran.
She could hear it—them,
running—stalking.
Squelching gurgles as they loped.
breathing—rattling,
chest chackling,
as mushrooms blossomed out of their throats.

Skin oozing, giving chase.
Her scent now on the wind,
she jumped into the clear calm lake
disrupted by her swim.

They crowded along the shore
and stopped at the point of tide.
She turned back to watch in horror
when she reached the other side

→»

They stood stock still as roots they grew
—defined through every face,
Their eyes turned black, then pooled,
as caps and lines then took their place

Hair floating down, feathers to the ground,
before the crown began melting away.
Beginning the slide, of their outer hides,
flesh in some faux kind of flay.

The black, it flowed down to their toes
as the stench of rot filled the air.
Their heads fell back as the stalk did crack,
rising from their guts like a Maypole at the fair.

Clouds of black and foul slime on the ground
as the spores fell like snow all around.
Frozen, she stared at plight of her town
where nothing familiar was to be found.

Fish jumped to catch the black flakes
As powder landed on water—spread as it sank
Dyeing dark, ripples from the wakes
of birds that were caught as they flew from its
banks.

And through the muck she saw them suck.
Tendrils now spread round,
from each pile that replaced a loved one's face
—slithered across the ground.

She scrambled up as they lipped and lupped.
Through the waves now spreading far,
she saw the ropes grasp and grope,
across the lake floor like a star.

She turned to flee, but there under the tree
slinked a bobcat already beginning to bloom.
It scratched and bit before having a fit—
she was free but facing her doom.

It burned and it itched—
spread oh so quick.
The pain now driving her insane—
The muscles ached
as they swelled in her face
and delirium racked through her brain.

Though she drooled as she sighed
Her throat was dry.
Breath from her lips grew harsher and harsher

-»

while the light grew brighter—brighter
Colors swirled round
as she fell to the ground.

Hunger pangs made her rise again
as she searched for a place to take shelter.
She found a barn that was dark and warm
and fell asleep next to a heifer.

Hours passed and she woke at last
no better for the rest.
She seemed to bow close to a cow
to suckle from its breast.

But soon it reared and kicked to strike
and drive her from its side,
as her teeth tore through its udder
gnawing as she ripped its hide.

The other beasts now roused to flee,
trampled her as they panicked.
Hooves stoving through sockets and goo
as her skull and limbs got flattened.

DUST

Her blood touched the air.
Through it, like fine hairs
the fungus spread and grew.
Over the hay and down in the drain
as it clotted then frosted and bloomed.

The darkness spread,
from each of the dead,
'til it covered the land and the sea.
No beast did it spare,
on the land or the air—
it soon even covered the trees

But the bones stayed,
cracked on display.
Hollow shells splayed instead of civilization
spread across atolls and glacial river flows—
no safety across any nation.

And then it was done, under rising sun.
The wind blew, but not a rustle was heard.
The ichor seeped and filled the deep—
none were saved, not fish or bird.

→»

A slimy coat on every boat
had the scent of hell gone bad.
All was gone ‘cept for the fungal arms
that now quietly embraced the land.

WRITER S MEET—UP GROUP

+

MICHAL MAHGEREFTEH

she enters with devious demeanor
    rattle walk and vile smirk tattooed
on lips thirst double espresso latte

wolfish stares and salty words
    yield years of sheer self-pity
forever whiner hungers for love

drains our generous vulnerability
    who no longer offers sympathetic ear
honest friendship, exempt of tenderness

COUNTEREXORCISM

\+

FEDERICO FEDERICI

vade retro!

my filthy fervourful imp!
bleed, jump through the fire hoop,
spin, copulate, shift, retort, as good
as you get, to my wishy-washy exorcism
with all the wit of your language's tips,
reject my rebukes for your many quips,
ergo low hum your ode, narcissus
eros et diem carpe! And—if you wish,
later—vade etiam mecum a bit,
favour him who with promises
beg thee, as you please
—me whipping thee, squeezing
thee from the muscles and bones,
dipping thee into this sip of Christ,
crossing me over thee,
blessing thee on my side,
I bear your mark in my voice,
I finally teach you the cross,

-»

L ESORCISMO CONTRARIO

+

Federico Federici

Originariamente apparso in Lùmina (Archivio Apocalittico Farsesco), *La Camera Verde, 2012*

vade retro!
   laido mio diavoletto con zelo,
sanguina, salta alla ruota del fuoco, rotea,
copula, trasla, ribatti colpo su colpo
all'inconcludente esorcismo
tutta l'arguta teoria delle lingue,
l'ammonimento alle tue molte
repliche di spirito, ergo
recita basso il tuo carme, l'eros
narciso e diem carpe! e – se possibile,
dopo – vade anche mecum un poco,
aiuta queste promesse di chi
ti implora, come ti pare – io che
ti fustigo, succhio da muscoli e ossa,
ti intingo al sangue del Cristo,
ti faccio un segno di croce

→»

COUNTER EXORCISM

I chase you in the fire,
I gaze from your eyes,
I cauterize you in capillaries,
I free you in the blood
through the needle,
I grind you on the black
iron, on the burden around my neck
of the cross.

da questa parte ti benedico,
ti segno nella voce, t'insegno
finalmente una croce,
ti seguo nel fuoco, ti salgo agli occhi, ti
cauterizzo nel capillare, nell'ago
dentro il sangue ti libero, rodo al ferro
nero, al peso al collo della mia
croce.

The Devil Said

Bruce McRae

The devil said "I'm what angels fear
as they stumble about in the Mystery.
I'm the six-foot crow of unplenty,
spreading salt on your back, licking your hair,
sniffing the fingers of the damned and dying.

"That's me in the nursery, an *influence.*
I'm the nursing home outside of visiting hours,
ticking blackened berries off my inventory.
The master of evil. Death's bitch."

The devil said "I am above and below you
and wear your penance for my shawl.
Never mind faith," he spat, "I'm the bull's bol-
locks.
To hell with prayer, I'm the jack of spades,
the last thing you'll see, a downpour of sharp
edges."
Becoming angry with himself the devil said,

THE DEVIL SAID

"Come fall with me my little chickens.
I'll show you the guts of your living.
I'll place these burning wires in your head.
Bow low and taste sin's splinters."

The more he spoke the less he said,
blistered, twitching, and red.
"I am the storm," he cried, clutching a fleshy fetish,
placing his perfumed fingers around my neck.
"The worms rustle for me in their temptation."

Struggling, I tried to turn away,
something miserable in my throat—rising.

In Defense of Mrs. Lot

+

J. Barrett Wolf

She was turned into to a pillar,
the story goes, for looking back.
Unable to close her eyes to a retribution
against the few who stalked in darkness—
not ten righteous men, said the angels.
not a woman...
Yet, what young child of Sodom deserved
to die by fire? What infant, brimstone?

Like the story of the flood.
A world castigated for the sins of a few.
Only Noah and his family saved,
to cower before the will of a god
so impotent that water, fire, and wind
could not rid the world of evil.
Lot's brave wife turned.
Stood like a column of the temple
unwilling to bend to a myth of capricious anger,

refusing to obey, refusing to depart
without so much as a look
at the dust and sulfur cast upon the plains.

She turned to salt, it is written,
salt of the Earth.
Tasting of oceans and tears,
without which there is no life.

Auditorium Shores

P.M. Covington

The thought floats into my mind
like the Colorado River,
that this wouldn't be a terrible
day,
or way,
to die.

Maybe the voices would say
"He was found sitting against a tree
    at Auditorium Shores,
a book of Charles Bukowski poetry
    open beside him.
Authorities confirm the presence of
    recreational drugs in his system."

And then,
like a sudden under-tow,
grey as early spring over-cast
I hear the voice conclude
    and it turns terrible,
"The official cause of death

Was a self-inflicted gunshot to the head."

Man, I gotta stop smoking spice while reading Bukowski alone in Austin.

How Do I Un—See

+

Coventree

Bloody night the time to call,
the witches cast their spell.
The cauldron belches putrid scent,
as demons are raised from hell.

Wings of bat swirl above
as feisty rodents scurry.
packs of wolves eerily howl
the drums beat in a furry.

Nude women undulate around a circle
enraging my loins raw desire,
called from sleep I stumbled to,
ogling them dance around the fire.

Concealed against a mighty oak,
lust engulfs me like a flame.
I cannot leave for fear of that,
I never see them again.
How could I return to a restful bed,

close my eyes and try to sleep?
The beating stops and silence falls,
their bodies raise into one great leap.

Within the circle its clear to see
rising up from within the fire.
A giant buff male glistening sweat,
crazed women calling out their desires.

Bats are screaming, Ravens fly
into the immortal flame.
I watch as he takes them all
never seeing them again.

A Family Affair

Richard Schiffman

The ears and the eyes had spent the better part of
a lifetime,
dwelling on the same head without ever
noticing one another.

Then one day, unaccountably, they quarreled. The
ears said to the eyes, "We have been hearing
rumors about you for years."

The eyes replied, "We searched and searched, but
you were nowhere to be seen."

The ears shot back, "You didn't write, you didn't
call."

The tongue wagged, "You looked right past me
like I wasn't there."

The ears pricked up in indignation, "You only
saw what was right in front of your own
nose."

The nose sniffled, "Ditto, ditto."

The eyes replied, "We didn't have the benefit of
hindsight."

The neck chimed in, "You made me twist and

turn like a freaking marionette."

The eyes asked, "Do you think I have eyes in the back of my head?"

The head said, "Thank God for small favors!"

Matters were quickly spinning from bad to worse.

The ears were growing weary of the loose tongue.

The tongue blamed the mouth for opening its big trap again.

The mouth accused that twisted ringleader, the brain.

The brain denounced its own madcap thoughts.

The thoughts said the senses were driving them crazy.

The tongue babbled, "The devil made me do it."

The eyes and ears cried, "Ditto, ditto."

The devil could not be reached for comment.

But his spokesman issued the following statement, "It is the policy of His Satanic Majesty to leave families to their own devices."

An Eerie Coldness Enters

James Piatt

As rain drenches the windows of the old farmhouse, I watch, in my mind, umbrae running through the halls searching for silhouettes of the past. The moon, an orange dullness, seeps silently into the room where I sit in terror. I gaze into my cache of terrifying memories, and see the face of a person who recently passed on to that evil place and wonder if the silvery streaks in the mist upon the windowsill, contains his terrible message to me.

Outside, the trees are shivering, naked from the winds of fall, and winter's gales. The rainstorm batters the old farmhouse, making the roof creak and moan. Only single sunbeams sneaking through thin apertures in dark clouds enter through misty windows to warm the icy atmosphere.

I am terrified that the coldness I feel is a premonition. I am afraid that a cold malevolent messenger—the specter of impending death—is pretending to be rain, battering the other side of the door.

CROOKED RITES

✝

BARON HENDERSON

A Poem Inspirited by the band Ghost

You call on me to sow a crooked rite
by the moon's full and evil shining light.
I say yes, let the acts be done.

The lady enters to watch the scene,
let all present open the gates of hell.
You call on me to sow a crooked rite.

The dagger is wielded by the horny priest,
revealed of cloak enters the twisted beast.
I say yes, let the acts be done.

The members hail the blood rights of Satan,
the lady smiles the sinister way.
You call on me to sow a crooked rite.

CROOKED RITES

Lucifer grants his blessing,
black candles burn as smoke fills the chamber.
I say yes, let the acts be done.

Worship the master of free thought,
the horny priest gives the damned signs he ought.
you call on me to sow a crooked rite.

The Devil seals dark fates sown,
drink from the fridge cup, cum into your own.
I say yes, let the acts be done.

Uplifted, imbued by the special power of mind,
tonight was rebellion, independence from Grace.
You call on me to sow a crooked rite—
I say yes, let the acts be done.

BAPHOMET

+

NEIL RAINN

I must admit that I'm a fan
(although I know it's incorrect)
Of the archaic term "Mohammetan"
(Wrong, as though they show respect)
To the Prophet, he was just a man
So "Muslim" (Submitter) from "Islam"
(Submission's) more correct.

Like how "Baphomet" first came
from the sort of trend you get
when scribes use distant, different names.
In this case, again, from Mahomet—
first appearing when some made the claim
that the Cathars, of "Carcasonne" fame,
who the Catholic Church saw as a threat
worshipped him in sickening rites.

BAPHOMET

When, in fact, a vegetarian feast
honoring an unfleshly light
led by men and women priests,
without any churchly wealth in sight,
was more their line. And this just might
have made the church look to the East

in such of details for their lies
(Since the Eastern heathen hordes
Had been already demonized:
The Daily Mail still use such words).
Then, once Cathars were despised
It could be more easily rationalized
to kill them for our loving Lord.

If something works, do it again.
So, when the church saw Templar Knights
collecting wealth and power, our friend,
Baphomet, had his name in lights.
Once more, and once again, used to lend
the justified crusading ends
that make the means of murder "right."

-»

This Baphomet was no goat, instead
the Templar Knights worshipped a cat
or else a reliquary head.
Kept by a cross on which they spat,
the head they kissed, or so 'twas said
in reports which lead to trials which lead
to the fiery jacket—the hemp cravatte.

Having been purged with stake and noose
The Templar Knights, of course, dissolved—
or went underground and on the loose.
Certainly, legends sprung and evolved.
One said that, in Scotland, they fought for the
Bruce (The Pope had sided with England. They'd
need no excuse for getting the Knights of the Tem-
ple involved).

Whether they died or went underground
The Templar Knights, and with it that name
continued to circulate, gaining renown.
In "histories" making spurious claims
that can read like a lunatic's rantings writ down,
or the plot of a plagiarized book by Dan Brown—
Then once more Baphomet's significance changed.

BAPHOMET

Alphonse Louis Constant—"Eliphas Levi Zahed"
Was a magician and author who wrote
a series of books (in their time widely read)
who, influenced by a classical quote,
said goodbye to the Templar's head
and drew from an Egyptian deity instead
which took the form of a goat.

A goat headed human, wings in its back
with a five pointed star incised on its brow.
While Levi repeated the old myths as facts
his new myths meant Baphomet looked like this
now.
Partly now female–undeniably stacked—
but with phallic staff and snake charming act
and words on their arms, written down:
"Solve" and "Coagula";
split up and join.

Baphomet, to Levi, was a mystical blender.
Hence the breasts on their chest and the snake from
their groin to signify union of binary gender.
With everything both sides of a single coin,
with their own special forces but all things con-
joined. That message was Levi's agenda.

→»

This creature, he said, was seen as the Devil,
of the kind that led covens in orgiastic rites.
That was true, Levi wrote, but this Goat wasn't evil
and when it led wild witches on their Sabbat nights
they were practicing ways from the Pagan prime-
val, seen as Satanic sorcery by the medievals
and described now as diabolic delights.

Something from Levi's imagination
in merging together the profane and the holy
struck a chord with and provided a clear inspiration
to a later occultist named Aleister Crowley.
Perhaps due to Aleister's infatuation
with "Cumming Together," from mere masturba-
tion to buggering neophytes slowly—
lewdly described by old Uncle Al,
Baphomet spread out further on the cultural scene.

And then Anton LaVey, Satan's best pal
And consummate showman, came up with a
scheme to found his own faith, in which to corral
weird loners, and Rayndians, and Suicide Gals
took the goat's head as it's meme.

If that account of that Church seems quite bitchy
it's also quite true, and they and I don't agree.
But while my own ways are druidic and witchy
The Satanists do some things that are pleasing to
me. If not Anton's lot, then at least one group which
he gave inspiration, though in some ways they ditch
the thoughts that went with his vocabulary.

They're The Satanic Temple,
and you'll say that you
Have not heard of them,
but you have and they're great.

They're the ones that fought for a Baphomet statue
To defend separation between church and state:
The argument being you have to take that, too
if county courthouses or any of that crew
think Christ is okay to celebrate.

The Temple campaign to uphold and change laws
on progressive concerns using tropes from LaVey.
Like protecting our access to safe abortion
with Satan, or Baphomet, being their way
to outrage their country's Christian portion;
Humanist aims with parodic distortion

-»

in the style of Jack Chick, I would say.

Baphomet has travelled from Templar to Temple,
picking up traits in his wake.
From a scurrilous slur in a legal preamble,
before burning a saint at the steak,
to a banner for radical rebels and vandals.
Gods and Monsters are like that, there's many ex-
amples.
Baphomet was a spelling mistake.

A Macabre Dream

Sravani Singampalli

Fireflies in their perilous eyes—
humongous, their bodies.
Behemoth in their demeaner—
tempestuous was the wind.

Wine-red were my tears
crippled were their thoughts,
sprinting through the woods,
grisly things in my vicinity
jeopardized my life.

Breaking free from monstrosity
ashen-faced with cold feet.
I became downhearted,
lost in the bizarre world.

I tried hard to escape
those dark unfathomable eyes;
my life became a spine-chilling tale
howling sounds from behind.

-»

SATAN SPEAKS!

Thunder in the sky seemed
like temper tantrums
of a frustrated old man.

The Behemoths still chasing,
their teeth like white daggers
trying to taste
my cherry-red blood.

At last clutched in their hands,
their fingers resembling
the pillar-like prop roots
of a banyan tree.

I screeched hard with pain,
my heart beating at the
speed of a bullet train.

I closed my eyes,
praying to god,
to save my life;
reassured to discover my reality
as I opened my eyes.

PART V

SHORT FICTION

Those Baroques

+

R. Keito

I got out of the taxi to see the front door of my house was open just a crack. I threw some bills at the driver and ran over to the door. The driver honked and popped the taxi's trunk. Flustered, I went back, got my suitcase, tossed it on the lawn, and went inside—I barely got to relax or see anybody or anything for the week I spent in St. Pierre & Miquelon and now this.

Looking up, down, all around, the living room, the bedroom, my home office, the kitchen, the bathroom, the closet...nothing seemed to be missing. My coin collection that isn't really worth anything was in my sock drawer. My stereo and wide screen were there. I have a fake Japanese sword that sits above my fake fireplace—untouched. I don't think I have anything worth stealing to begin with. Even the pizza I forgot to eat before I took off to St. Pierre & Miquelon was still in the fridge.

Heading back to the bedroom, I figured out what it was. My mother's paintings. She had them since I was a kid, two velvet paintings of large barque ships. The normal black velvet background, the ships in misty greyish blue, stormy clouds above them on each of the paintings. When I was young they would give me nightmares, I could make out freaky looking faces in the paintings of those barques; I'd and toss and turn each night. My mom wouldn't take them down no matter how many times I told her I woke up in the middle of the night with the heebie-jeebies.

I never considered him my stepbrother or anything, but Zach must have brought the paintings over and dumped them on my lawn. Zach's dad, Benjamin, hooked up with my mom after my own dad had left us and went back to St. Pierre where he grew up. I never really got along with Zach and him as his dad was kind of a jerk. So, after my mom had passed on, I guess Ben told Zach to get rid of those creepy velvet paintings, dropping them off when I wasn't home. They're all I have left to remember my mom by since Ben screwed me out of anything else of my mother's belongings.

The next day I went back to work at Jitters

and everyone asked all the expected questions. How was St. Pierre & Miquelon? What did you do there? Do you have any photos to show us? I made coffee for some of the regulars; they didn't ask me any questions. None of them noticed I was even absent.

On my break, I made a flat white and sat outside. Across the street I saw someone taking two large frames into the pawn shop across the street. They struggled to open the door with their elbow while carrying the frames and managed to prop the door open with their foot. After five or seven minutes, they came back outside without the frames and I could see who it was.

Their name was Cheryl, or Shannon, or Sherrie, I can't really remember now. Though I know quite a bit about her, I hadn't seen them in about four years. She was a friend of Alejandro who used to work at Jitters some time back. He and I got friendly and he told me he thought that Cheryl, or Shannon, or Sherrie and me would really hit it off, but she was in Paraguay, or Peru, or Bolivia volunteering and would be back in a few months. A week later I got a postcard from Cheryl or Shannon, or Sherrie. So I replied with a letter. We kept writing back and forth all the time she was in Paraguay, or Peru, or Bolivia. From her letters, she seemed like she had a brain and she had rode down to Paraguay, or Peru, or Bolivia on her motorbike, which tickled my interest more so.

She finally came back home and we met in person. We met for coffee, then went to a Jamaican restaurant I like to haunt. Her letters were always interesting. She told me she wanted to move to a bigger city because this one is too small because she keeps running into people she went to college with, people she used to work with, old lovers—it was time for something new.

I felt no connection whatsoever. After we hung out she told me to call her sometime. I never did. She went to the trouble of sending me a letter in the mail. Points for effort, but I just didn't feel anything between us. And if I'm going to be honest, what turned me off the most about Cheryl, or Shannon, or Sherrie was that she "talkssh like dissh and it'ssh hard to undersshtand when she sshpeaks."

Cheryl, or Shannon, or Sherrie left the pawnshop and I crossed the street and went inside. There were my mother's scary velvet paintings behind the counter. Someone was already dabbing a price sticker on one of them.

I asked how much they were and the old man behind the counter said “These just came in!”

“Yes, how much?

“One fifty.”

I didn’t know how to reply and simply stared at the freaky faces I always saw in those baroques; the old man said *each.*

I walked back to Jitters to finish my shift, wondering if my childhood insomnia was worth dealing with the police over or just forking over the three hundred dollars, or hoping my mom would understand if I did nothing about it.

The Samhain Show

Edward Ahern

Brunstella sighed, wishing she had gone into dealing drugs. “I can’t move the cauldron.”

Griselda patted her sister’s shoulder. “Of course you can, dearie. Just use a spell.”

“I’ve only got magick left for one spell. I’m not blowing it on rolling a rusty iron pot out into the woods.”

“Then hire a troll.”

“With what? Nobody pays us for spells anymore, they’ve all got miracle cures from pharmacies.”

Griselda’s voice hardened. “It’s the Samhain sacrifice, sweetie, we swore to observe it.”

Brunstella grabbed her cane and stood up, joints creaking. “If we cut the baby into quarters, we could just use a stew pot and freeze the left overs for next year.”

“You know better. It has to be a whole, live baby girl, unbaptized. Unbaptized is easy to find these days."

"Yeah, but not so easy to boil. The last one puked in the pot and it took me three hours to clean it out."

Griselda leaned forward to whisper in her sister's ear. "Do be cautious, younger sister. You know who is listening."

Brunstella's laugh was harsh. "When's the last time we saw her? Eighty years? I think she's wagging her infernal booty elsewhere. We're obsolete."

Griselda slapped her, mottling the wrinkled skin of Brunstella's cheek. "Never doubt the Mistress! Just do as she ordered us."

Brunstella muttered but stiffly lowered herself back down to think. If magick was out she'd have to rely on cunning. *I could have done better for myself,* she thought, *a shill or a prostitute, but look where I am.*

Then an idea struck her and she got up with a groan and hobbled down a dirt track that lead away from their cottage, then forked left onto a gravel road for another half mile, eventually reaching a cabin. She walked up to the door and yelled inside.

"Tom, you sober enough to talk?"

"Get away from me, you miserable hag."

"Don't be like that. I need you and your tow truck."

"The last thing I did for you gave me shingles. Go away."

"No, seriously. I can give you erotic visions like a sultan never had."

Tom snorted. "Get out of the dark ages. I've already got four bookmarked porn sites, all free."

Brunstella wouldn't be put off. "Okay, how'd you like to get wasted on the nectar of the gods?"

"Like you knew how to get it." But his tone had changed, and Brunstella knew she had him interested.

"It's an old family recipe. All you have to do is move something and I'll give you enough divine booze to stay blasted for a week."

The door cracked open, and a blotchy, bleary eyed face appeared. "Move what?"

"Just a big old stew pot. I need it to go into the woods, then a few weeks later to be lugged out.

"How big?"

Brunstella's first instinct was to lie, but she knew he'd find out anyway. "Maybe four hundred pounds."

"That's not a pot, that's a hot tub. Make it enough booze for two weeks."

Brunstella didn't hesitate. "Done! It'll be ready for you day after tomorrow, when you come to move the cauldron."

She hobbled back down the gravel road but stopped just before the turnoff onto the dirt track and went up to a one wide trailer that hadn't moved or been improved for a quarter century. The make-shift wood steps up to the door were almost rotted through, and she stepped carefully, then knocked. "Craig! It's Brunstella. I got a deal for you."

"Get away from my door or I'll be the one cursing you."

"Now, now Craig, I think I can take that contaminated moonshine off your hands. Maybe even pay you a little."

Craig, who considered himself an unappre-ciated cinematographic genius, cracked open the door and peeped at her. "It's got turpentine spilled into it, you old biddy, nobody could abide the taste."

Brunstella smiled. "Yes, well by the time I've added in herbs and hallucinogens, it'll taste like nectar. You still got it?"

"Yeah." Craig opened the door all the way and let her in. "How would you move it?"

"I'll come by later on with a wheelbarrow." She looked around the room. Everything was gray, hidden under a half-decade of dust. Everything except a small desk with a lap top computer and sheets of paper. "Working on something?"

Craig's shoulders sagged. "I got an in at a studio, producer named Harry Beerstein owes me a favor, but I need a concept for a TV show, and my mind is farting bad scenarios."

That's when Brunstella had her second great idea of the day. She stood still for several seconds, thinking it through.

"You've been living so bad you might as well have been cursed, Craig, but I've got your cure."

"I doubt you've even got money for the booze."

"Hear me out. Reality shows are what everybody's watching right? We give 'em the ultimate: intrigue, hatred, nudity, promiscuous sex, violence, even human sacrifice."

"Hah?"

"The Samhain ritual, stupid. We do a bunch of episodes leading up to the sacrifice, shoot it all on your hand-held camera, hire our neighbors in for dirt wages—hell, some of them would do it for free—it's got everything. You just need a watcha-callit- trunk line.

"Log line. Jesus, Brunstella, it just might work."

"Don't bring him into it. Of course it will. How's this for a log line? 'Hidden witches corrupt their town for devil worship.'"

Craig had started pacing back and forth, stirring up dust. "Close. But you and Griselda are toad ugly. Nobody would watch you with or without clothes."

"Don't worry about that. We'd use some of our local sinners for the sex scenes and nude dancing. For the climax episode we'd rent an unwanted infant…"

Craig warmed to the idea. "Then shoot the parents getting remorse and showing up at the ceremony and getting beaten and cursed. All staged of course, but what reality show isn't? Yeah, I like it."

They talked excitedly for another hour, Craig tapping possibilities into his lap top. He was so worked up about the project he gave Brunstella the contaminated hooch for a hair restorative ointment.

Darkness was creeping in as Brunstella limped down the dirt track to their cottage. She knew she couldn't tell Griselda, not yet anyway. Griselda was the conservative witchy equivalent of Opus Dei. As she entered the cottage, lit only by firelight and candles, Griselda was skinning a cat.

"Ritual?" Brunstella asked.

"Supper," Griselda replied. "What about the cauldron?"

"Taken care of. You and I are going to Craig's tomorrow with the wheelbarrow and picking up two cases of poisoned booze. I doctor the booze and give it to drunken Tom, who'll use his tow truck to carry the cauldron into the woods."

"We don't have money for that, and you've got no powers right now. How'd you do it?"

"Grace and kindness. Don't worry, it's done."

"Tom's apt to die or go crazy."

"Yup."

"Okay. Supper'll be ready in a half hour."

Griselda and Brunstella picked up and doctored the moonshine the next morning and delivered it to Tom. Craig showed up at their cottage two days later. He was afraid to go up to the cottage door and called out from down the path. "Brunstella!"

She heard his third yell and came out, putting a finger to her lips, then walking with him into a shaded grove. "What news?"

"He liked the idea. Said it was fresh, edgy. But he doesn't know you. Or trust you. He needs some footage to show what we can do."

Brunstella nodded. She appreciated doubt and suspicion. "Your camera and mic working?"

"Sure. What are you thinking of?"

"Tom's hauling a cauldron for me. You and I go with him into the woods, along with that skank girlfriend of his. You're filming all the way through. I do some smoke and haze mumbo jumbo over a bottle of the booze and give it to them. They'll start drinking, it's what they do. Then you shoot whatever else they do, truck bed, hood, front seat, whatever. There'll be enough Spanish fly in the bottle to kill the bull it was meant for."

"What if they die on the hood?"

"Doubt it, those pickles left cucumber behind a long time ago, just keep shooting. They're apt to drool, so get close enough to show the spit bubbles. Then I step in, yell some nonsense, and administer an antidote."

"Antidote?"

"Just an emetic, ilex vomitoria. But their spew should be good footage."

"I can't do that to Tom."

"Tom does it to himself all the time. Besides, he probably won't remember. And you've got the almost porn that could get us the show."

"That's pretty vile."

"I know. Fun, isn't it?"

And so, it was scripted, and it was done, edited. Tom displayed remarkable staying power and inventiveness. Craig was just clever enough to put the footage on a website with one-time, protected access, so his close friend couldn't shop the idea around and double cross him. Harry Beerstein called back two days later.

"Brilliant work, Craig, brilliant. But I need a copy so I can show it to the right people."

"That's great, Harry. But first things first. I need you to option the concept for say thirty grand. I've drafted and registered a little something I'll send you. As soon as we're in binding agreement I'll be glad to send you a tape for circulation."

Harry got peeved, yelling that Craig was grievously lacking in talent and that his ancestry was sub-human. But once Harry saw that his bullying was having no effect, he quieted down and agreed.

Craig went into town and bought a burner cell phone, then turned around and drove down the dirt track to Brunstella's cottage.

She saw him coming and hobbled out. "Do I need to curse him with boils?"

"Nah, he's sending the thirty thou, enough to get started. Look, here's a cell phone. I'll show you how to use it."

"I can't. We hold to the old ways."

"And I'm not going to shag my ass down here every day just to talk with you. Considering how it's used, I'm pretty sure this is an invention of the devil."

Brunstella had thought Craig through. So long as he was straining for ego gratification and money, he'd be an adequately bad boy. But once he'd arrived as a movie maker, Brunstella was going to have to short leash and muzzle him with a nice disfigurement curse. “So what’s next, Craig?”

“Beerstein will put together a promo piece using some of our edgier footage and shop it around to investors. He hopes to get the up-front money commitments a few weeks after that. You’re going to have to tell Griselda then.”

Brunstella spat yellow. “I know.” As they kept talking, they walked in a circle out to Craig’s one wide and back. As they re-approached the witches’ cottage, Brunstella’s insides felt like they’d curdled into corpse rot. “Somethings wrong,” she told Craig. “Get out of here. Now. I’ll call you on that flapdoodle.”

She hobbled gingerly up to the cottage door and entered. Griselda faced her, both arms akimbo, broken into odd angles. Witches can’t cry, but Griselda’s sweaty skin and rheumy eyes told of great pain. “What did you do, you clapped out whore?” Griselda demanded.

Brunstella hobbled one step toward her sister, then stopped. Something was sitting in the chair next to the fireplace.

“Yes, Brunstella, what did you do?”

The greasy voice poured over Brunstella like burning oil. Which was okay, really, because she did the same thing recreationally. "Mistress."

"I leave you two to quietly corrupt into dust and you cause trouble with my new projects."

"Mistress?"

"That bulbous letch Beerstein is shopping around a Samhain concept for a reality show. That's something just between us girls. I've devoted too much time corrupting this nation to have it interfered with by Amateur Hour."

The Mistress' words were soft pitched and calm and coated in venom. Griselda had started to whimper. Brunstella's mind churned desperately, and she pulled together fragments of what Craig had told her. "Mistress, you have been so busy damning the mainstreams that you haven't had time for the tributaries."

The hand on the arm of the chair turned into a claw, mostly blotchy blue. "Explain yourself."

"Just market segmentation. Griselda and I are traditionalists, we understand the part of the viewing audience that still watches televangelists."

"So?" The word dripped acid.

"The Samhain reality show will apparently condemn wanton, infernal behavior, but will show it in such an attractive way that the religious will be curious. If they're curious they're halfway to you, a large group you're not reaching with your current programming."

The thing in the chair smiled. It wasn't pleasant.

"Brunstella, you wart plantation, you're onto something. Needs work of course, some demonic script writers, ads in church bulletins, that sort of thing. But yes, maybe. You're coming to Hollywood. But I can't have anyone as ugly as you working for me or having a lead role. Hold on."

Brunstella dropped to the floor writhing in pain. Everything, even her teeth hurt like heaven. When she stood up again she was thirty something with fully working, reasonably attractive parts. "Thank you, Mistress."

The thing in the chair glanced at Griselda. "A theatrical career requires personal sacrifices Brunstella. I'll need to shut down your little operation here. Are you willing to dump Craig and abandon Griselda?"

Brunstella considered the alternative. "No problem."

Kicked Out of Hell: A Case of Stolen Identity

Eskarina Weatherwax

It was a dark and stormy night.

—The sound of a record player needle scratching across a vinyl groove—

Wait…Let me start over.

It's the usual damp, foggy Coos Bay, Oregon midnight. I'm in my house on the hill, looking down on Highway 101 toward the east side of the Bay. The paper pulp mill upwind is stinking the air with the smell of sulfur, reminding me of home, only without the heat. I'd been stuck here, on the Outside for six years. After wandering around the North American Continent for 2 or 3 years, I'd finally landed here on the Southwestern Oregon Coast.

I don't know how I missed the sound of footsteps. There was a knock at the door. The the doorbell rang. More insistent, loud knocking followed.

Can't they wait?

Dammit.

Why won't they let me eat my goat cheese and crackers in peace!

By the time I reach the front door, I realize that the exposition has lasted too long. I made the rules. I guess I can break them if I want to.

"Yeah?" I end up looking down at a black cat. How could she ring that doorbell?

She—I think the cat's a "she"—winds her way in past the door like she owns the place, blinking her green eyes at me. She is wearing a red collar studded with rubies, with a larger, faceted one in the center of her neck. Her owner is rich? And I notice two cute little white vampire teeth peeking from her lips as she vaguely smiles up at me.

"You don't remember me?" she purrs, (of course, she'd purr).

"Hmmm. You couldn't be that…" I rack my brain trying to remember.

"Just as I thought."

She moves out of the entryway and into the living room, making straight for my favorite cushy armchair.

"Goat cheese. I love goat cheese." She reached out a paw, swiped some cheese and started licking her foot. "You forgot our date."

"DATE!? We had a date?! TONIGHT?" I squeak.

She turns and pins me with a glare. "Yesss. How could you forget?" Her vampire teeth look less cute this time, as she gives me a pissed-off look. "I'm the best pussy you've ever had."

"So. Um. I've missed our meeting." I pointedly leave out the idea that we could have had a real date. "Did you find out anything? I've been exiled since 2014. I thought I was the Head Devil of Hell, and what happened? They kicked me out! All because some power-hungry devil-underling stole my identity."

"*Meow*…well. I did find out there is no information on this side. The lesser demons I've crossed paths with have nothing to tell me, even under severe 'enhanced interrogation techniques,' what the CIA euphemistically calls torture." She swiped some more of the goat cheese. "We're going to have to go back home somehow, and solve your identity theft problem on site,"

"Like THAT's going to happen."

"Come on. You know you're the Head Dude of the Place. Stop acting like a wuss. Besides, you know Hell like the back of your hand, since you are the one and only architect. What happened? Did you lose your memory, or did your spine turn into spaghetti? You've been acting demented, like your brain has melted."

Hmm. She had a point. The shock of getting ousted out of my own Kingdom had thrown me for a loop. I'd been in a deep depression ever since. That, and all the fresh cool air Up Here was killing me. "So, how do you think we're going to get back in? Walk through the front door?"

She snorted in exasperation, flexing her claws. "Look. I'm tired of all this."

With that, there was a shimmer on the chair. She stood up and shape-shifted into a gorgeous woman—red, slinky dress with cleavage down to THERE, long black shiny hair with well-placed fashionable glossy red-black horns growing out of her head, still wearing her ruby necklace around her neck. Her red lips were shiny with lipstick as she smiled with seductive annoyance, showing white pointy vampire teeth. She—WAIT! I finally remember her name—her True Name—Hezicat. I felt as though she'd physically slapped me. My brain snapped back and my memory unclouded. A plan started to take shape. I hoped my lightning reflexes were coming back.

"So. You're finally almost back to your old self! Almost too late!" she said as she stepped from my chair and sashayed to the center of the room. Turning to me, looking at her blood red manicured nails, she continued, "You know, you can't let this situation go on for much longer. The lesser devils and demons are making a mess of things without you keeping them under your thumb. Just look at all of the crap that's happening around us Up Here. In fact, one of the obese, orange-faced lesser demons with a 'Dennis the Menace' wig has escaped, and his stupidity and incompetence is causing massive chaos, not just here, but worldwide. He's been promoting himself as the 'smart guy,' who gets things done. He's stolen your best line, 'Believe me.' All he's managed to do is wreck things, create more turmoil by throwing his considerable weight around, all of his businesses going terminally bankrupt—including the government he's supposed to be in charge of, turning everything he touches into shit. He's making Hell look like some luxury spa destination in comparison to what's going on Up Here."

"Ok. Just let me think for a moment." Floating up from my awakening brain, I see an image of the Map of Hell—the place I'd built over the millennia. I recall there was an old, secret hidden door I'd installed for a "bolt hole" out of Hell, an escape hatch, just for me alone, for "just in case" situations. It was so ancient, that nobody else in Hell knew about it, and I'd almost forgotten it myself. I looked at Hezicat and pursed my lips in thought. "You know, there's top secret exit I know about. We could sneak in that way. Then, the two of us can get to the bottom of the mystery of my stolen identity."

She smiled, "Now, Stan, you are getting back to your old wily-self. Your ruddy complexion is coming back. Your horns don't look so dull. Your tail is starting to perk up. You are beginning to look your old handsome evil self." That was quite the compliment coming from her.

I gave her a leer, "We'll have to navigate to New York City, though. But I know we can teleport ourselves via portkey with no problems. The escape hatch entryway is in the basement of 725 5th Avenue in Manhattan—some 'gold tower-skyscraper' I think. We can glamour ourselves in disguise right through the front door. We get back to the Inferno I call Home, investigate the situation, find the culprit, and I can exact my revenge."

"We can administer appropriate punishment" she said, clapping her hands with almost too much enthusiasm. "Well, don't just stand there. Let's get this show on the road!" Her smile grew even wider, canine teeth gleaming. "All it took was a slap upside your head to get you back to the old Stan I know and love-hate."

With our plan taking form, we have to get to one of the local portkeys, which is located in Eugene, Oregon.

We go through the house, checking to be sure that it's sanitized of all devilish evidence, packing up any magical items we may need to have with us. I stash everything into two expensive black leather attaché cases.

Hezicat and I stuff everything in my black Mercedes Benz sedan and lock up the house. I drive north, across the McCullough Bridge, headed to Eugene, 125 miles away.

It takes us about 2 hours. We go along lodgepole pine-lined Highway 101, turning northeast on Highway 38 at Reedsport. The road hugs the banks of the green Umpqua River as we pass through Pacific Northwest rainforest, breezing by the rural towns of Scottsburg, Elkton, and Drain. When we reach the junction of 99 at Interstate 5, I start traveling north down the Willamette Valley.

"Do you remember where this portkey is located?" she asked as she picked through handfuls of Chex Mix road trip kibble, eating just the salted pecans and pretzel sticks.

"It's in the new law school building on the University of Oregon campus. I moved it from the old law school building when the school relocated. Appropriate, don't you think?" I smirked.

We both chuckled at the snarkiness of my idea.

I parked the Mercedes in a residential area, where it won't get a ticket and we walked back to campus. Glamouring ourselves to look like law school students, we went in through the front doors and took the stairs up to the fourth-floor section of the law library. The library isn't as empty as I'd hoped it would be, but I'm willing to put up with a few inconveniences just so we can travel efficiently to Manhattan.

"Where did you hide the portkey?"

"It's in the men's room on the southeast side of the building." We made our way there, and by the door to the men's room, Hezicat stopped me with a hand on my chest.

"We have the beginnings of our plan to get back, but how are we going to manage our way through Hell to do our investigation? You know our glamour won't work there. And we'll need to get a computer so I can do some investigative back-tracking to find out who the hacker is."

I smiled. "I've got that figured out. It's easy. Because the secret back entrance opens up to one of the largest computer centers in Hell. There should be no problem! Otherwise, we will have to be extra careful not to be seen. Unless things have changed since we've been Up Here, most of those sent to Hell are demoralized enough to ignore anyone except their direct tormenter-demons. Just wait until you see where we come in." I twitch my eyebrows provocatively, as if I'm Stephen Colbert.

She nodded with an interested look, her long shiny fingernails adjusting the large central ruby on the necklace, so it rested in her subclavian notch as we opened the door to the restroom.

"It's over there, in the stall furthest from the

door. All you have to do is stand on the toilet, and push on the flush lever with your foot."

One at a time, we activate the portkey. With a disorienting "floosh," I pop into the busy lobby of the Lexington and 59th Street subway stop.

Hezicat appears a few second later. "Cleverrrrr Portkey!" she purrs with her snide vampire grin.

Nobody notices as we glamourize ourselves to look like we are well-off business people. I'm in a bespoke black silk suit with a red tie—with a flame motif, of course—and she is wearing what any rich, successful woman would wear: a Prada red silk jacket and skirt suit, with 6-inch Manolo Blahnick black spike heels.

Black attaché cases in hand, the two of us exit the subway and make our way to the golden tower. We walk in as if we owned the place, check in at the Security Desk—where we are both given badges—and move toward the bank of elevators. "It's been a long time since I've seen you, Mr. Natas, and you, too, Ms. DeVille. Just head on by and go right on up."

Given his OK, we head to the farthest elevator from the front door. We get in and as the doors close, I push the Stop button, wave my fingers in a secret sigil, pop open the secret invisible panel, and push the newly revealed key that says DOWN. The elevator drops with stomach-lurching force, finally stopping at the -666th Floor. Once the door opens, we step out into a dark, small room.

I light my left index finger to find red mops, brooms, and buckets that say "Property of Hell" painted on the outside, and on the handles of the mops. All sorts of cleaning products line the shelves on the walls: strychnine, Round-Up, cyanide, Uranium 238, cobra venom, ricin, Japanese puffer fish, Black Widow poison, sarin nerve gas, blue-ringed octopus venom, poison-dart frog venom, polonium, arsenic, Oxy-Clean, and Amway all -purpose cleaners. I know that Hell can never be too clean.

I see a red glow showing under the door in front of us, that leads out. "I hope they haven't made any new architectural changes to *My* Hell. Wait until you see my most recent addition. I was pretty proud of this before I got evicted." I open the door. Hezicat stands just behind me. We are at one corner of a giant cube farm, laid out over acres of space, all lit with red LED tube lights. The cubicles have red fabric on the walls. "Can't be too modern.

Welcome to the Corporate Level of Hell." I say, guiding her in with my hand at the small of her back as we step in out of the custodial closet.

I close the door behind us, and all signs of a door vanish, except for the handle, and a metal sign on the door that says "Cleaning Products."

"Now, here we can find an open cube, and unused computer terminal to start our search for the culprit. We just have to be careful that nobody notices us."

Skulking down the aisles, Hezicat and I manage to avoid being seen by the infrequent demon-supervisors checking on their "employees." We usually can hear them as they approach. They like to crack their electronic laser-whips as they walk from victim to victim, getting off on the threat of torture and the sounds of pain they inflict on their "employees." The demons come by randomly to torture the "inmates" with hot whips and branding irons. Corporate Hell is for "special people," those who were in upper management, administrators, CEOs, stockholders and the Koch Brothers. "None of the corporate drones are ever sent here. Those sent to Corporate Hell are so used to working without breaks, hours at a stretch in their former lives, now feel accustomed to working for eternity—the only difference is the high temperatures with the sulfur-smelling a/c.

"Well, Ms. DeVille," I snark, "Let's go find an open computer—or maybe you want to visit the whole IT department, servers and all?"

She turns to me as we walk, "Did you keep the Original Hell-Levels, and just add these new ones?"

"Sure. Hell is becoming an urban sprawl. This is two levels above the "Lawyer Level of Hell," I grin. "I needed to make room for more of the 'deserving.' After all, my Kingdom is a growing enterprise."

"So. You remember Dante and Virgil's visit?"

"Of course. Once I got my head on straight back there. I remembered everything Down Here, from All Time. I'm starting to feel better, more like myself, now that the air is up to a decent temperature and has a healthy stink like it should."

We manage to find an empty cubicle. Posted on the red fabric wall behind the computer monitor were org charts, a map of this specific Level, along with a poster that said, "Arbeit Macht Frei"—"Work Makes you Free." I snarl to Hezicat,

"Those stinking Nazis STOLE MY saying to put over the entrance of the Auschwitz concentration camp! You DO know they have their own special place with special, heinous 'therapy' Down Here?" She nods her head with a knowing, malevolent look.

I pull back the red office chair and gesture for her to have a seat. There was constant piped in music, the selections rotating from elevator music, to Nickleback, Creed, Justin Bieber, Lawrence Welk, Jonas Brothers, Neil Diamond, to Ted Nugent, and, last but not least, Barry Manilow. Other than that, all that could heard was the clicking of keyboards, and the random screams of those being tortured.

She clicked the computer to life, and the monitor flashed awake. "You know what you're looking for?"

"Not exactly. I just want to check to see if the delinquent left any digital foot prints." I take a seat in the chair to her left. She opens the operating system files, looking for any tell-tale evidence that someone had been messing with the identity files—MY identity files; but nothing shows up. After clicking and mousing for 90 or so minutes, she finally hisses in exasperation, "I'm being led in circles. There's no way I can get anywhere using one of the regular computers on the Corporate Level network. I have to get into the server system to see if I can track down any evidence that someone mucked around and altered your identity data."

"Well, I know that we are at least 6 miles away from the Server Room. Since this level is active 24/7, you and I will have to figure out a way to get to the IT section on this floor without being seen. Can we do it?"

"Of course we can," she says. Her canine teeth take on an exceptional white shine in contrast to her blood red lips. She closes the computer down, turns her chair towards me and stands up. "Do you think that anyone here is looking for you?"

"Not that I know of. We didn't hear any alarms going off when we opened the Janitor's Closet, did we?" I look up through my eyelashes, listening, psychically sensing demon energies. "Nope. Nobody seems to know that we are here. I don't want them to start any celebrations by trying to kill us. I'd like to track down the scumbag who did this to me, and murder whomever it is and send them to that

'Special Level of Hell,' you know, that level where 'the roaches go in, and they don't come out?' That place that's technically known as Oblivion?"

Hezicat fingered her ruby necklace. "You know we've been lucky so far. None of the regular crews of demons have cruised by while we've been here while I've been trying to hack into the server. You know our luck might not hold forever."

"Yeah, that crossed my mind, too. Come on. Let's get our sh—tuff together and see how long it takes us to cross this corporate cube farm."

It didn't take us anytime at all to collect ourselves, so I stuck my head out of the cube doorway to check to see if the coast was clear. A squad of red and black demons with laser batons was crossing about half a mile down the aisleway, surrounding a new screaming "convict" with their arms restrained in a straitjacket, force-marched to their assigned cube-cell. Other than that, everything appears quiet. "What are these guys getting paid for? They aren't DOING anything! Where is the noise of torture and mass mayhem? When I get back in charge, things are going to be better…Or really worse for those who have been sent here by my loyal agent, Karma! Whoever has tried to take over from me, has a lot to learn about hard work! MHGA: 'Make Hell Great Again!' And yes, that fat-hog-of-a-lesser-demon stole my slogan!" I turn to Hezicat. "Let's roll. It sounds pretty quiet out across the acreage, so let's make a run for it."

If someone were watching us, they would hear sound effects like that tinkling xylophone from the old TV cartoons, where the characters are sneaking around on just their tippy-toes.

We zip down the aisles as fast as we can, all the while carrying our black leather attaché cases. The closer to the center of the acres of cube farm, we get more activity that we see and hear. The size of the demon-groups increases from squads to brigades, each gang herding new "residents" to their assigned spot. We stop to catch our breath, luckily we side step into an empty prairie dog cell.

Hezicat turns me to face her, "I think things are heating up, more so than usual for Hell. I thought I heard you accusing the a-hole who stole your identity of being a lazy S.O.B. We've still got about 4 or so miles to cross. I have an idea, but do you have a better one?" How irreverent can she be? Since she is my familiar, I know that "Snark" is one of her middle names.

"Ok, I'm game. Tell me your idea."

"Let's travel on the ceiling. You know, nobody looks up. They have their attention focused on the prisoners, and aren't looking around. There's no reason for the guard demons to expect anyone to come and rescue the folks who bought and paid for a one-way trip to Hell when they sold their souls."

"Ummm. Good point. If we shrink ourselves small enough, the size of the magical force field around us will shrink down too, and not be as noticeable."

Keeping an eye out for more demon-troops, we sidle our way over to one of the drywall surfaces in a wider hallway on the edge of the cubicles. We wave our hands in mysterious magical gestures and sigils, even though we are out in the open. Hezicat changed into her black cat form before changing into a large Black Widow spider with a tiny ruby necklace, all the while still holding on to a tiny black attaché. At the same time, I change into a black bat, then morph into my black spider-form, about 2½ inches in diameter. It's a good thing that both of us can run with 7 legs, the 8th leg holding our attaché cases.

It doesn't take us long to climb up the wall and onto the ceiling, which, thank Me, is made of tiles, and not that popcorn stuff that used to be so popular.

"I like your tiny horns, Stan. You know you are kind of cute as a spider." She smirked at me seductively.

"You know we don't have time for this. Being this small takes us a while to cross the last 4 plus miles to the server-room."

"Yes, but just think, we can focus on traveling, and take breaks when we need to without having to constantly watch out."

The lights never go out on the Corporate Level of Hell. The red fluorescents stay on forever. And sure as anything, nobody—no demon, no new inmate, no nothing, not even the dust—looked up, ever. Hezi and I manage to have a picnic about 2 miles in to our crossing. I lash down my attaché case with spiderweb, open it and take out two fresh ham sandwiches on whole wheat.

"Why Stan! How thoughtful. How did you ever guess I liked ham?"

I drummed my seven legs on the ceiling

tile. "You and I know EVERYTHING about each other. You KNOW that." She just blinked all eight of her spider eyes at me. We finished our sandwiches, dropping whole wheat breadcrumbs on the carpet below us. We unlashed our cases and continued our crawl the last two miles. Good thing that Hell doesn't mind dust and hanging spiderwebs, they just focus on cleaning the areas on the floor.

After what felt like a month, we reached the wall of the Data Center and climbed down. We knew it was a safe area, all of the traffic on the floor was at least a mile away from us. We take extra magical care while reversing forms since the servers are very sensitive to sorcery.

Hugging the wall, Hezicat and I skulk around the outside corners of the room, looking for the entrance. "Well, it looks like there is no visible doorway. Do you have an idea how we can sense it out?"

"Maybe. My necklace has some magical properties. Keep an eye on it as we walk around this time." We didn't have to go far. About half way down the wall, two of the rubies on either side of the large, central gem started to blink. "Here. Take your fingers, and you can trace a warm line where the door should be." As I move my fingers down the line, I hear a click, and a black metal doorknob pops out of the red wall. Hezicat turns the knob, opens the door, and we see acres, miles of computer servers. A space larger than what the outside containment walls would lead someone to expect. "Come ON! Get inside, before anyone notices!" She grabbed my hand and jerked me inside, almost bumping my head on a server rack. She shut the door with a quiet "snick." The black door knob sunk back into the door, which disappeared.

"You DO know, that this center ruby has a magical nanochip computer hacker powers? It's going to tell us which server to get into, which hack to use, and most of all, who the guilty party is who stole your identity and then kicked you out. It will also warn us when someone knows that we've gotten into the right server, and will protect us from getting discovered. Now, all I have to do is walk systematically around the space here, and let the Ruby do the talking."

I am amazed. I thought I knew everything about my Familiar, but apparently not. I follow Hezicat up and down the data farm aisles until she stops, points, and kneels at a server. Letting out a Yowl worthy of any cat fight, the central Ruby flashes with red-laser intensity. Hezicat telepathically connects with the server's digital guts.

"Malphas! It's MALPHAS!" she shrieks. "Your second in command! HE'S the one who had you kicked out. He's been pretending that he's YOU all these years since you've been gone! He thinks that he can 'Out Dark' the real Prince of Darkness!"

"That sneaking son-of-a…By Beelzebub's Britches! Why that conniving, butt-kissing, motherfu…" Foaming at the mouth with such rage, I can't even swear right!

My head stretches up to hit the ceiling. "I thought I could trust him!" I try to raise my arms in a threatening gesture, but I'm stopped by the asbestos ceiling tiles.

"Shhhhhh! Stop your yelling! We might have already drawn his attention down here!" She pats my arm in a soothing way. "OMS!"—Oh My Satan.

"So, Malphas is a power tripping monster. Now you know who your real enemy is. Let's get going and get him out of your throne so you can clean up his mess, get rid of that little prick demon, the Orange Menace and the rest, straighten up Hell, so it can run like the efficient torture machine that it is."

Once again, Hezicat has given me the psychic "slap upside the head" to get my emotions back on track. I look at her, "Are you sure you aren't the real Satan who runs Hell, instead of me?"

"Oh, Stan, always with the compliments."

Malphas. That old schemer. I'm sure, with his skill at building towers and deception, that he WOULD have been the force behind all of the BS on the Outside, including the little fat demon-prick who has been screwing with the United States at all levels. And I fell for Malpah's sneaky manipulation, gaslighting and lies. Of course, that's his true nature, since he was born right here in Hell. Now… time to nab him by the "nads."

I laugh my ass off. I know *just* the final solution to put an end to Malphas! As someone said somewhere, "Revenge is a dish best served inferno hot." I snicker to myself; of course, an evil snicker.

I grab Hezi by the arm. "Come on. I'm going to draw Malphas out, and make him come to ME. He won't suspect anything. He'll probably think that I'm vulnerable, a loser since it was so easy to kick me out this time. He believes that he still has the upper hand. Little does he know."

We pick up our attaché cases and find our way out of the room housing the server ranch. I start making my way to what I think would be a likely spot for Malphas to ambush us. "Let's see if he's still using my Throne Room. I'd guess that he'd want to use my furniture, so as to maintain the illusion that he's the 'real Satan.'"

Hezi and I make our way to the central elevator. I push the button to go up to Level 9, which rockets up from floors 665 to the 9th floor, popping our ears and causing a trickle of blood out of our noses; normal humans would probably feel their brains slide all the way out. As the door opens, I make a gallant gesture for Hezicat to exit. "Level 9. Cosmetics, perfume, lingerie…" She waves her attaché case at me. "Now, to get our act together. The Road ends here."

I guide the two of us to one of the anterooms outside my Throne Room. Just as I assumed, nobody is in what would be considered to be a luxury suite in any hotel. Time to prepare myself to regain my place in Hell.

Opening my attaché case on a gold brocade upholstered sofa, I begin digging through my supplies to get to my chosen weapon. Wouldn't you know, my case is bigger on the inside than it looks. I start with the stuff on the top: a pair of red suede goat-hoofed shaped high heeled shoes, assorted bull whips, a red lightsaber, a copy of the *Satanic Bible*, a live goat, a 6-foot high marble statue of Baphomet with an inverted Pentacle carved on the marble plinth. There is a small jar of menstrual blood, a box of communion wafers, several wads of clothing that had been shoved into the case, an extra-long black dildo—large sized, anatomically correct with balls (*I'll talk to you later*)—a hardcover copy of Salman Rushdie's *Satanic Verses*, (I've always wanted to read this just to see how accurate it is), a cat-o-nine tails, a Dungeons and Dragons Dungeon Master guide book, a red MAGA baseball cap, and a .38 revolver with silver bullets.

I continue to reach deeper into the case, throwing the contents behind me into the room. There are Blu-Ray copies of *The Exorcist*, *Alien*, *Predator*, *Legend*, *The* "Me"*'s Advocate*, and John Waters' film *Pink Flamingos*. Going deeper, I find an old box of condoms, a Gay Pride button, an AC/DC CD *Highway to Hell*, a brass Aladdin's wishing lamp, Tom Riddle's wand, a 10 pound bag of

Kingsford charcoal, a full-sized vintage French Guillotine, a pitchfork, a snakeskin bag of dice, a black top hat, a woven willow handbasket (filled with goodies for Grandma), a black silk villain's cape lined in red satin. Digging deeper, I find a printout of the lyrics of "Kiss the Go-Goat" by Ghost.

Next, a cardboard box of Underwood's canned deviled ham, various Medieval torture devices (including a rack and an Iron Maiden), and a plate of fried Rocky Mountain Oysters.

The room is getting cluttered as I throw more stuff behind me. Deeper into the attaché case yet, I pull out a battery-powered boombox that plays both CDs and cassette tapes, then more music CDs with bands like Iron Butterfly, The Damned, The Cramps, Black Sabbath, Young Gods, Bauhaus, Siouxsie and the Banshees, Sisters of Mercy, The Dead Kennedys, Captain Beefheart, The Grateful Dead, Metallica, The Beat Farmers, and Nirvana—I'm into 80s music, obviously…

I finally find the object of my quest, the reason I've kept digging through the contents of the leather case: last, but not least, a maximum-sized Super Soaker that I've specially loaded with holy water blessed by Pope Ratburger-Benedict 16.

Hezicat nods appreciatively at the Super Soaker. She winks, and says, "I think that should do the trick. Malphas won't know what hit him."

"Oh, NO! I *want* him to suffer." I give her a sharp look. "The holy water will set his skin on fire! Let's check to see if the Throne Room is empty or not. You know that he wants his followers and sycophants around him to constantly stoke his ego. We may have to wait for me to set and bait my trap."

Hezi opened one of the doors to see if the Throne Room was clear. She dropped her attaché case near it and shimmered into her cat-shape. She cocked her head in the direction of the open door and trotted in to inspect the space for us, sneaking behind drapes and furniture to scope out the soon-to-become magical battlefield.

While she is busy, I put on the black silk top hat, the black cloak, take Tom Riddle's wand in my left hand as I heft the full Super Soaker under the other arm.

"It's clear. Let's set up as fast as we can."

Hezicat shapeshifts back into her voluptuous woman-persona, and we claim the Throne

Room for ourselves. My first order of business is to take the wand and cast a circle widdershins, with my throne in the middle, the Super Soaker in easy reach. The circle glows red, setting a laser-border. "Open the door, sweetheart." She goes to the main gold encrusted door and pushes it open, and then dashes across the red circle to join me.

I shout with my best invocation voice, filling all of Hell, "Hey Stupid! You thought you could win this one. Well, SURPRISE. I'm BAACK, Malphas, you LOSER. You can't fool me. Time to face the music."

Off in the distance I hear a small roar of anger before the pounding sound of a herd of little demon-pig feet galloping toward us. He's coming, and he's pissed. Not only that, but he's bringing his entourage to witness what he assumes will be my demise.

Malphas stops at the door, smoke coming off his hoofs; his minions crowded at his back.

He smirked. "So Stan, You think you can come back as the Head Honcho of Hell, do you. And you think that little red circle will protect you? HA! Looks to me like I can just get you in an easy wrestling hold and throw you out of that protection zone."

"Well, Malphas, if you think it's so easy, why don't you come and get me, shit for brains."

He can't help himself. He charges into the room and crosses the line of the circle. With a simple gesture, I raise the red light up, creating a half sphere dome of red light. I make a second gesture, and the circle-dome becomes brilliant white light. This catches Malphas's attention. "So, you think you can simply trick me, 'Satan-Boy.' You are so dumb that I could get you kicked out of your own country, and now you think you can beat me with a magick circle." He walks over to the dome, expecting to just go through, but as soon as he tries to move through, the wall of white light bounces him back; he hadn't expected this. Enraged with surprise, he gallops around the edge of the lighted dome, trying to punch through the energy-wall with his shoulder. "HEY!" he decides that he can turn this to his advantage. "So, it's just me against you, and this weak girly pussy. You can't even die by yourself; you are such a wuss."

I stand my ground. "That may or may not be so, Malphas. You've let all of the lesser demons loose to the Upper World. You think you are such a stable genius, so tremendously smart, but in case you haven't noticed Hell is a fuckin' mess on all levels. You are a chaotic egomaniac."

If a demon could get redder with anger, I watched Malphas become garnet colored as a frown and smoke puffed out of his ears and his horns.

I take a step and grab his fat red neck. "I thought I could trust you. As my second in command, that you had the same values as me. Hell is meant for spiritual therapy of souls who deserve to learn that evil is not a life-goal. Hell is not meant to be designed as a place for you to stroke your ego, saying 'I'm the King of Hell.'" Malphas didn't give a shit. He figured there was nothing I could do to punish him; he figured he would always be in charge.

I let his neck go, and he starts bouncing on the wall of the energy dome again, as if he was popcorn. I reach down for the Super Soaker, first cocking it to fill the magazine, then tucking the back end under my right shoulder. "I bet you didn't know that I could kill you."

He stops in his tracks to the right of my Throne. He has this incredulous look on his face. "You can't kill me. I'm immortal."

"Yeah, that's what all the assholes say."

I aim the forceful stream of holy water at his abdomen, then his chest, and finally his head, spraying the solid liquid power-stream of holy water, drowning him in deadly juice. As soon as the holy water hits his skin, he is screaming in agony, "Stop! Stop! No! NOOOoooooooo."

He tries to avoid the stream, clawing, pawing, trying to wipe the fluid off. His skin starts smoking with sulfur stink, blue flames are burning from his ears and out from the top of his head. He starts shrinking and screaming. I'm reminded of the melting scene of the Wicked Witch of the West in the 1939 movie, *The Wizard of Oz*.

"Burn, you stupid SOB, Die! Get the fuck out of my kingdom. I COMMAND YOU TO GO TO THE OBLIVION OF THE OUTER DARKNESS, WHERE YOU BELONG. WHERE NOBDY KNOWS YOU OR REMEMBERS YOU!"

I turn to Hezi, who is calmly standing next to me. "A fitting demise for a narcissist, Hezicat, don't you think?" I say above the agony.

The screaming torture is contained in the light dome, but as soon as Malphas' body flashes into a mushroom cloud, the Dome implodes, a vortex of energy clearing the Throne Room of all Malphas's ashy debris and negative aura-shit. Hezicat and I stand there, letting the wind do its worst, our clothes not even affected by the force of the gust.

"Are tornadoes the model for the modern-day vacuum cleaner?" I asked. All that is left to show that there had been any sort of magical confrontation is the red circle mark on the floor of the room.

I fold my arms across my chest, surveying the freshly cleaned up space. Hezi gives me her side-eye and a snarky vampire-toothy grin. "I don't like what he did with the décor."

I wave my hand, and the throne grows longer, and becomes the size of a loveseat, complete with red velvet cushions. "Would you mind joining me, Miz Hezicat? There is room enough for two."

She renews her black cat form, and jumps on the cushion next to me, and curls up. I wave my hand in a magical pass, revealing an end table with her favorite—goat cheese on a plate. "Why, thank you, Stan." She takes an appreciative nibble. "You know how much I enjoy goat cheese."

There is a crowd of demons, monsters, and other strange looking characters at the entrance to my Throne Room. They are cheering and talking all at once. "Thank Satan, you are back, Stan! We missed you," All of Hell's denizens were glad I was back. "The place wasn't the same without you! The infrastructure was turning into shambles. All of the lesser demons who usually do the dishes, maintenance, and custodial work, were escaping Up There, and nothing was getting done! They weren't even capturing those folks who think evil is cool, and bringing them down here to work for us on a permanent basis. Upstairs was becoming more like Hell on earth, as if Hell was just a second -class tourist destination."

Beelzebub popped open several cases of jeroboams of Champagne, and Belial passed out crystal flute-glasses. Some of the demons were rude, preferring to drink right from the bottle.

"Let's not get too absorbed in all of our celebrations just yet. I'd like to send Pythias, who is very familiar with liars, to capture that orange-faced lard tub. The very one who has been causing all sorts of unnecessary grief up 'Top Side.' I don't want to forget to thank you all, demons and monsters, for welcoming me back with open appendages. Once Hell is back to normal, you all can get back to work!" I snapped a whip with a *CRACK!* that I found tucked in the back-seat cushions of the sofa

I lean in towards Hezi, "And YOU, my Sweet, you and I will celebrate later in our own 'special way.' Maybe I'll even give you a new nano-collar, perhaps studded with diamonds this time. I couldn't have come back to The Inferno without all of your help."

"But Stan, don't forget that I have that extra career Upstairs, moonlighting as Christine McConnell on that *Curious Creations* TV show."

"Thanks for the reminder!" I smirk at Miss Hezi, and kiss her paw. "Before I forget, I want to make sure we invite Santa down for a drink or two. You know he gets all busy preparing toys and goodies for his global Christmas Eve trip. Be certain you are here to join everyone in thanking all of the dyslexic kids who have been writing their toy lists to me. Since we want to keep tabs on all of the bad people, Santa's list of naughty and nice kids will make it much easier for us to collect future members of the Hell Community, wouldn't you say?" Hezi leaned over and affectionately bit me on the neck.

She looked up at me, with her usual seductive and smug expression, "Didn't I tell you more than once I am the smartest, best pussy you've ever had?"

Acknowledgements

I would like to thank Fredric Z. Saunders and Daniel Cureton for their assistance with elements of the story.

Sources + Images

Front cover:

Koltyrina, Lia, "Black and White Retro Photo, Woman Demon, Devil. Girl with Horns, Effect of Toning—Image." *Shutterstock*, ID: 462013339, https://www.shutterstock.com/image-photo/black-white-retro-photo-woman-demon-462013339. Accessed 19 July, 2019.

Back cover:

Gerasimova, Katja. "Demon Goat Baphomet with Sacred Occult Eye. Satanic Goat Head. Binary Satanic Symbol. Vector Illustration Isolated. Tattoo Design, Retro, Music, Summer, Print Symbol for Biker Black Metal Themes—Vector" *Shutterstock*, ID: 1105872050, https://www.shutterstock.com/image-vector/demon-goat-baphomet-sacred-occult-eye-1105872050. Accessed 1 Aug. 2019.

Fonts

Licensed Usage

Chequered Ink Ltd. "Beast of Rage." *Dafont*, https://www.dafont.com/beast-of-rage. font. 12 Aug., 2017. Accessed 1 July, 2019.

Hansen, Chris. "Requiem Font." *1001fonts*, 2017, https://www.1001fonts.com/requiem-font.html. Accessed 1 Oct. 2019.

Morison, Stanley. "Times New Roman." *The Times*, 1931, https://docs.microsoft.com/en-us/typography/font-list/times-new-roman. Access 1 Aug. 2019.

Literary

Back cover quote:

Goethe, Johann von. Faust. "31." Trans. Bayard Taylor. Boston: Houghton Mifflin, 1898. Online access: *Monologue Archives*, http://www.monologuearchive.com/g/goethe_001.html. Accessed July 1, 2019.

www.ingramcontent.com/pod-product-compliance
Lightning Source LLC
Chambersburg PA
CBHW071411100726
47908CB00004B/1136

9781734006711